In Quest of a Vision

In Quest of a Vision

Sr. Isolina's Own Story of Gospel Servanthood among Puerto Ricans

SISTER MARÍA ISOLINA FERRÉ, M.S.B.T.

Translated by Sister Yolanda De Mola, S.C.

PAULIST PRESS
New York • Mahwah, N.J.

All photos in this book were provided by the author.

Cover design by Tim McKeen.

Library of Congress Cataloging-in-Publication Data

Ferré, Isolina.
  In quest of a vision : Sr. Isolina's own story of gospel servanthood among Puerto Ricans / María Isolina Ferré : translated by Yolanda De Mola.
    p. cm.
  ISBN 0-8091-3692-9 (alk. paper)
  1. Ferré, Isolina. 2. Missionary Servants of the Most Blessed Trinity—Biography. 3. Church work with the poor—Puerto Rico. 4. Nuns—Puerto Rico—Biography. I. Title.
BX4705.F419A3   1997
271'.97—dc21
[B]   97–9980
                                                                        CIP

Published by Paulist Press
997 Macarthur Boulevard
Mahwah, New Jersey 07430

Printed and bound in the
United States of America

CONTENTS

Translator's Preface *1*

Isolina: Story of a Vision, Preface *3*

The Vision *5*

The Vocation *14*

The Novitiate *37*

The Missions *53*

The Playa *82*

Afterword *112*

"There were moments when she physically stopped street fights between Blacks and Puerto Ricans. That's something for a woman. They were tough kids, but she was fearless."

Testimony of Father Joseph Fitzpatrick, S.J.
1992 Andrus Award Presentations Documentary, AARP

TRANSLATOR'S PREFACE

This relatively brief account of the life and work of Sister Isolina Ferré makes no mention of the many honors she has received. At the risk of offending her modesty, I would like to list a few of the fourteen colleges and universities from which she has received honorary degrees in recognition of her years of selfless ministry in behalf of so many: Fordham, Queens College, and Bank Street College of Education, all in New York City; Marymount; The Catholic University in Washington, D.C.; St. Francis and St. Joseph, both in Brooklyn; Fairleigh Dickinson in New Jersey; Holy Family in Philadelphia; and Yale. She has also been honored in her native Puerto Rico by the Interamerican University as well as by the Catholic University of Puerto Rico in Ponce.

The leadership roles she has filled are legion. They include vice-chairperson of the Milton Eisenhower Foundation and membership on the Governor's Council on Drug Addiction, the Council on Juvenile Justice and Delinquency Prevention, and the Task Force on Mental Retardation.

In 1980 Sister Isolina was U.S. delegate to the World Conference of the Mid-Decade for Women in Copenhagen, and in 1971 she was guest lecturer at the International Congress of the Inter-American Association of Studies in Criminology held in Caracas, Venezuela.

Sister Isolina has written extensively on the subject of community organizing in its many aspects during her years of service in the United States as well as in Puerto Rico.

Outstanding among the more than sixty awards Sister

Isolina has received in the United States and in Puerto Rico are the Albert Schweitzer Prize for Humanitarianism from Johns Hopkins University in Baltimore, the National Puerto Rican Coalition Life Achievement Award, and the John D. Rockefeller Foundation Public Service Award for Community Revitalization from Princeton University, in New Jersey.

Undoubtedly, the God who called Sister Isolina Ferré so long ago to serve him as a Missionary Servant of the Most Blessed Trinity will himself be her exceedingly great reward. For those of us who have known and admired her, she remains an inspiration and model in our work for others. In gratitude to God for her life and work, I offer to English-speaking readers this, her story.

Sister Yolanda De Mola, S.C.

Isolina:
Story of a Vision
Preface

*I*believe that, to be effective, every undertaking must be guided by a vision. I do not refer to a simple objective to be attained, or to some small and limited goal, or to short-term satisfactions; I refer rather to a clear awareness of tangible possibilities that are profoundly rooted in the heart and mind of each person one meets along the way, regardless of race, creed, or social or economic class. It is an awareness of the elements that are *life-producing* for a person, and the ability to bring together human experiences in a mosaic that can give meaning and fulfillment to human beings.

A vision ought to be evaluated and well grounded; *it must give and preserve life.* It ought to help one to perceive profound meaning in the lives of other human beings, and to search for whatever may be needed to bring that meaning to full realization.

This book deals with such a vision. It has taken shape ever so slowly within me with the same care and authenticity with which a flower, a butterfly...even a child, are formed. It is a vision, which, upon maturing, has a face that can be easily recognized; a face that I was able to discern through the years at every step along life's path. It is the face of those who lack all material things but who enrich us with the interior treasures they carry within. It is, in the final analysis, the face of the poor.

In writing this story, I began with the most remote memories I could recall. Sources I have used for information include some issues of the bulletin, *El Playero (Ponce);* the many interviews and talks I have given; even some data written about my life in newspapers, especially *El Nuevo Día (San Juan)* from October 21, 1990 to January 13, 1991.

My most profound and eternal gratitude go to my friends along the way who, although they do not have the face of the poor, have helped me to clarify my ideas and put them in order, especially Rosario Ferré, María del Carmen Monserrat Gámiz, R.S.C.J., and Medelicia Madera Acosta.

—*Sister Isolina*

The Vision

*I*t began to take shape in my mind and heart from childhood days. When I recall those years, I marvel at the mystery of Divine Providence that transformed my life. It was in Ponce that I first became conscious of poverty, of marginalization and helplessness, while at the same time developing a love for the needy and an understanding of their capabilities.

My parents, siblings and I lived very happily at Number 13, León Street. We had everything: love, care, respect... and lacked nothing in the way of material goods. We enjoyed domestic help, always good and obliging; and there was Pellín, an excellent chauffeur, who was to become a central figure in the raising of my consciousness. Pellín was very fond of me because, as he tells it, he "heard" me being born. In those days babies entered the world at home. On the day of my birth, September 5, 1914, he was in the garage and he heard my first cry before anyone else. They gave me the name Isolina after my father's only sister.

I recall that after Pellín dropped my father at home each day, he would invite me to climb into the car and go for a ride. Often those rides would be to the homes of his girlfriends, and they were many. He had girlfriends everywhere, for he was sociable and quite a ladies' man. Thanks to Pellín, therefore, I had access to a different class of people. I remember that we used to visit a section of Ponce located behind the church of La Milagrosa near the Club Deportivo (Sports Club). Pellín would park the car in that general area. I would enter a house where there was a small table, some benches (there were no chairs), and perhaps a rocker. I would sit down and his friends would give me sweets or coffee with milk while Pellín was served black coffee. I used to love hearing the conversations of these people and enjoyed their amiable ways. This proved to be a very profitable experience for me, because it caused me to ask myself why they wore such plain clothes, and did not have the kinds of chairs or other comforts such as I had at home. I began to notice the difference between Pellín's friends and my father's friends.

Adults seemed quite taken with me. I was talkative and chubby and seemed to please others, so that they were readily inclined to talk to me. Because I was so pudgy, my brother Joe used to call me "balloon" which caused me great merriment. I was always welcomed in people's homes. When Pellín would take me for a ride, he used to buy me goodies. One of my favorites was *bacalâitos fritos* (codfish fritters). At times he would take me to the town of Juana Díaz because there they made them extra tasty. Pellín would purchase them and later Papa would reimburse him. We would get out of the car and chat with people. In this way I came to know another type of person, especially those who made the codfish fritters—which, by the way, were the best ever. To share with others was a good experience for me.

Many persons worked in my home. I related to them to the degree that I could, since they were always very busy and I was quite young. My mother was growing old and her health was not as good as it had been when she was raising my siblings. Because of her illness, she often went to the mountain town of Adjuntas to rest. My siblings were off at school, and so I spent a lot of time with the employees at home.

The laundry area of our house was located in a small building at the far end of the yard. I used to go there to play with a little monkey that my father had named Moncho Reyes on the day he brought him home. This was the Puerto

Rican's derisive nickname for our then governor, Mont-gomery Riley. He was so lacking in management skills that people were always making jokes about him. The people who did the washing, the ironing, and the cooking were very pleasant, and I enjoyed a close relationship with them. In dealing with them I was getting to know another world, one that was becoming very attractive to me. Their surroundings and their lifestyle were very different from those to which I had been accustomed.

The other people who attracted my attention were the vendors in the marketplace. From time to time the cook would take me to the plaza to do the daily food shopping. There I came to know the greengrocers and learned how they spoke. While enjoying their sense of humor, I watched how they dealt with people. If I behaved myself, they would give me presents, such as rag dolls. They were lively and cheerful people. I was fascinated as I listened to them jok-ing and telling stories.

I remember that once a year my mother used to invite the little girls from the local orphanage to our home. On such occasions she would gather us all together and say: "Get ready to clean the house, wash the dishes and shine the silver...everything."

Her preparations would turn the house upside down.

On one occasion I asked her, "Mama, why...? Is it some-body's birthday?"

She answered: "No, but we have invited the children from the orphanage to spend some time with us."

"But, Mama, they're orphans," I answered. "Why so many preparations?"

And she answered, "They are the same as you. The only difference is that they don't have the good fortune to have a mother and father as you do and so we are going to share with them as if they were part of the family."

And that is what we did. These visits took place once a year. We would prepare the best home-made sweets: ice cream, and cakes. The Sisters of Charity used to bring thirty or more little girls from the orphanage, and we served them. I still remember my question: Mama, why do we have to do this for them, when they are only orphans? This is how I began to understand that all of us were equal; that there was no difference between us; that we were all children of the same Father: of God.

My parents frequently received visitors, and they were of all kinds; I remember one in particular. When I was just eight or nine years old, if memory serves me, we had a visit from Theodore Roosevelt. This took place at our house in Adjuntas during the summer. Before his arrival, Mama said: "Since Teddy Roosevelt is coming to see your father, you have to lock up Teddy (our dog) so that he won't be running around loose." This we did, and hours later Mr. Roosevelt arrived. The adults settled on the porch and we youngsters went out to the yard to play with the children our guest had brought with him. Thank God Teddy, our dog, stayed where we had locked him up.

When they left, Mama noticed that I looked sad and asked me: "Isolina, what's the matter? Didn't you like your little playmates?"

I answered: "No, one of them is a show-off; he thinks his father is the greatest thing on earth and he was boasting all the time."

My mother looked at me and said: "But why does that upset you? You too have a father who is even greater, because you are a child of God. Therefore, nothing and no one should make you unhappy because you enjoy the dignity and respect of being a child of God." I think that, from that moment on, those words began to take root within me

in a much more profound way than I could have at that
time realized.

I recall the Feast of the Three Kings (January 6) with great
nostalgia. It was an extraordinary day on which we received
many gifts. We would place every one of our presents out on
the porch so that all who passed by might admire them. On
that day Father used to welcome his employees and their
families to our home. They would sit in the parlor and chat.

On one such occasion, my mother introduced me to one
of the children and said, "Listen, Isolina, didn't the Three
Kings leave a present for this little girl?"

I answered: "Oh, yes, yes, of course!" And I ran to my
room to get an old doll I had received the previous year.

But when my mother saw me return with it, she said: "Oh
no, not that one; the nice one in the blue dress, the one you
have on the porch."

It hurt me terribly to have to give away my new doll, since
I had hardly any time to play with it. Later my mother
explained to me: "When you give a present to another person, always give the best, not what is left over from before;
remember that they too are your brothers and sisters and
you must give them the best that you have."

My mother was always very generous with the poor and
with all those whom she saw in need. Our house was
located next to the Plaza del Mercado (marketplace) so that
from our porch we could see everyone coming and going.
One day a man who had no legs passed by our house, strug-
gling to move himself along on his stumps. My mother
began to engage him in conversation, asking him what had
happened to him, where he lived, etc. I don't know how she
did it, but a few days later, mother had managed to get him
a small platform on wheels so that he could sit and move
himself along with ease. She also got him an assortment of
sewing materials together with a box in which to place

them so that he would have something to sell and be able to earn some money. She never lost an opportunity to explain her concerns to us and, little by little, I began to understand that people's needs can never be ignored. What I saw her do, I realized, must be done for all in need. As the years passed, these experiences with my mother inspired me to seek employment for other handicapped people in the area so that they might have a chance for a better life.

My father also was a generous person and a tireless worker. He was always jovial...the sunshine of our home. And he was zealous for our happiness, especially at Christmas and on the Feast of the Three Kings. He would bring us very special gifts: parrots from Venezuela and exotic and delicious sweets. I remember that he used to take walks in the afternoon, and sometimes a group of beggars would be waiting for him on the street. In those days beggars had the custom of going from house to house every Saturday asking for alms. My father used to open a small wallet and distribute money to them, and then stay with them a while, engaging them in conversation. They grew so accustomed to him that they waited for him almost every day. *It was not a question of giving because they asked, but of sharing.* Father knew the names of every beggar in Ponce and, although one might be crippled and another otherwise maimed, he would never refer to them by their disabilities as others might, but always referred to them by their names. I learned those lessons very well.

We used to spend summers in Adjuntas, a marvelous place in the interior, mountainous region of the island, where my life was enriched by knowing and sharing with all types of people. In June we would undertake the big move of the year. My father used to rent a different house every year until finally he built his own. We were an extended family made up of parents, brothers and sisters, servants, and friends of the family. Our house was surrounded by a small plot of land where Father grew vegetables and raised some chickens. I recall one of those summers; I was ten years old and my best friend was a little shoeshine boy named Cariño. He taught me how to ride a bicycle and explore all the areas of Adjuntas. Thanks to him, I came to know every neighborhood and mountain in Adjuntas.

My parents did not approve of my riding a bicycle, but Cariño lent me his and taught me how to ride it. At first he would hold me, and when he felt I could manage by myself, he would leave me alone. I felt like a bird that had been freed as I dashed up and down the street until one day I came down a steep hill. The bicycle gathered speed, but Cariño had forgotten to teach me how to brake! I was faced with two alternatives: go straight ahead and land in the river, or crash against one of the houses. For the first time in my life I had to do some quick thinking, and I opted for the second alternative, resulting in a broken bicycle and skinned knees. I took myself to the pharmacy where they attended to my wounds. When I returned home I said nothing to my mother, but the next day was Sunday and we had to go to Mass. All went well until the moment of Consecration and my mother whispered to me "Kneel down!" As I did so, the spontaneous look of pain on my face gave me away, and I spent the next two days in bed. In the last analysis, the fall was not totally tragic, because my father ended up purchasing two bicycles, one for Cariño and one for me.

A significant aspect of this phase of my life was my growing awareness of how much the poor knew. I learned a great deal from Cariño, and this influenced me. I understood the importance of learning from others, especially from the marginalized. We often take it for granted that only friendships within our own social class are worthwhile. It is only when we come to respect the dignity of all people that we become aware of those qualities that *give life* to human beings. Throughout my life I have learned to listen to people, and as a result have learned a great deal and gained great satisfaction.

To return to my childhood memories. Once a young boy named Guadalupe stood crying outside our house because his family had thrown him out of their home. He was living on the streets. (In those days there were many homeless children on the streets of Ponce. They preferred to live around the Plaza del Mercado or some other well-populated location.) We took Guadalupe into our home and brought him to Pellín who gave him a good bath. When the boy came out from the bathroom, we couldn't help laughing, and someone commented: "Where's the boy who went into the bathroom? This one's a white boy." To our great surprise, he had become a different color; the bath had lightened his skin. We bought him some clothes and dressed him. He remained in our home for a long time, and we helped him in many ways. We had a large yard by our house where there was lodging for our employees. It was there that we provided shelter for boys like Guadalupe.

Years later, when I was already a Missionary Servant, I made a trip to Puerto Rico from the United States and on that occasion I saw Guadalupe who was then in the Merchant Marine. He came over to me and asked if I remembered him. He said he was one of the young people to whom we had given hospitality. On another occasion I met another young man who was born in the Cantera neighborhood and had become a policeman. Upon seeing me, he asked: "Do you remember me? I used to go to your house and you taught me catechism. You used to dress me like a shepherd for the Christmas plays."

During my childhood, a vision concerning values gradually developed within me. I came to see the worth of every single person as potential raw material in the formation of human beings destined to live life to the full. It was this vision that led to my vocation of serving the poor as a Missionary Servant of the Blessed Holy Trinity.

The Vocation

*"The All-powerful designer has a plan
of life for you, and each of your
days His mysterious Providence is
weaving all this into a work of incomparable beauty..."*

(July 14, 1933:] Fragment of a letter written to me
by Father Thomas Augustine Judge when,
while I was still very young, I began
to manifest signs of a religious vocation.)

"*I*solina, what would you like to do when you grow up?"

On several occasions, when this question was posed to me, I would invariably give the same answer:

"A dancer or a nun!"

Dancing fascinated me. I remember one day the question came up after a dance recital at the Broadway Cinema. I was about three years old, and had participated very briefly with a few simple dance steps. I was very excited, but I found myself faced with the dilemma of having to choose whether to be a nun or a dancer when I grew up. After a few years, I became painfully aware that my feet were not at all suited for the "pas de deux," and my heart began to be inclined instead toward the needs of the poor. I did not become a dancer, but instead a nun whose restless feet have never been still for very long.

I come from a traditional family where, as the youngest of

14

Sister Isolina's First Communion in 1920.

Sister Isolina in her school uniform at age 11 while attending the Sacred Heart Academy.

House on León Street where Sister Isolina was born.

Sister Isolina's parents: Antonio Ferré and Mary Aguayo.

The family's summerhouse in the town of Adjuntas.

Sister Isolina's family seated: Her sister Saro, Don Antonio (Father), Sister Isolina. Standing from left: Brothers Herman, Luis, Jose and Carlos.

The Motherhouse where Sister Isolina went in 1935. She used to call it "The Seven Gables." (Philadelphia)

Sister Isolina during her work at the Dr. White Community Center in Brooklyn, NY, talking to Puerto Rican families.

Sister Isolina with Francis Mugavero, Bishop of Brooklyn, while working at the Dr. White Community Center, 1965.

six, I was reared and educated within a loving atmosphere created by my parents and siblings. My father, who was of French ancestry, was a Cuban emigrant. He had started out as a mechanic, and took a correspondence course to become an engineer. My mother was born in St. Thomas, the place to which her parents, who were of Spanish extraction, had emigrated to set up a department store at a time when Ponce was undergoing one of its many periods of economic recession. My childhood was spent in outings with my parents and with Pellín, the family chauffeur. It was filled with fiestas, fun, and play, but at the same time, with quiet observation of my parents' acts of charity, especially my mother's kindnesses toward the least privileged in society.

My father used to enjoy taking us around the towns of the island, and en route would explain the geography through stories. Although he was a Catholic, he did not practice his religion faithfully in every detail. On a certain occasion, a friend, on his death-bed, asked my father to take his place in the Aurora Masonic Lodge, and he did so; he became a Mason so that the chain might not be broken. This upset everyone at home very much. With the passage of time, the Pope made my father a Knight of Saint Gregory because he had been a co-founder of the Catholic University of Puerto Rico, and he had to hasten as quickly as possible to sever his connections with the Masons. My mother was beautiful: tall, graceful, and strong. Although she later contracted *filaria* (a tropical disease), her bearing was always regal and gracious even when, to disguise her condition, she wore long dresses.

In 1917, I was enrolled in the Academy of the Sacred Heart which had just opened its doors in Ponce. Since they did not have many pupils, the Madames had asked my parents to enroll me, even though I was only three years old. The school was on Isabel Street which today is where the

Diocesan Seminary, Regina Cleri, is located. The Madames used to wear a habit that seemed funny to us: it was completely black and they wore strange-looking high black shoes. We used to think that they placed pebbles inside them as penance.

I was a very active child. I recall that one day in October of 1917 there was a strong earthquake while I was at school. All was very tranquil when all of a sudden I began to hear the older students screaming (I had not felt the tremor). Soon the mothers of some of the children were rushing into the school in housecoats and with disheveled hair to pick up their children. Everyone around me was screaming. Suddenly I noticed that the nuns were spooning out a green liquid which they were giving to the girls to calm them down. When I took a spoonful of the liquid, which tasted awful, it calmed me down considerably, and even made me somewhat lethargic. But I learned how to calm my fears without screaming. My older brothers, Joe and Luis, ran out of the public school they attended and went directly to the Liceo Ponceño to pick up my sister, Saro. They didn't give me a thought. Don Pedro Schuck Grau, the father of my little friend Olga, came to pick her up and, seeing me there alone with no one around to get me, lifted me into his car and took me home.

Those were happy, peaceful years in which I learned a great deal. Mother was my best teacher with her example of being a good Samaritan to all, irrespective of their stations in life. The Madames at the school used to tell us stories of the saints and other holy people, stories of their lives of sacrifice even unto death for the sake of Jesus. All that, together with my experiences with Pellín's friends and the employees at home, as well as the example of my parents, little by little served to prepare my heart to hear God's call when it came.

From those happy years, I remember the many times my mother would sit me by her side on the porch of our home on León Street. She would recite poems, pausing occasionally to chat with people who were going to or coming from the market close to our home. One time a lady passed by in great distress because she had several children and was unable to support them all. She said to my mother: "Please take my little girl." Mother did not hesitate to accept the child, and she became part of our family. We used to say the rosary with my mother in her room before a small image of Our Lady of Perpetual Help. When Mother died, my sister Saro kept the image for a while, and then it was given to me.

We frequently visited the shrine of the Virgin of Montserrat in the village of Hormigueros. We traveled there in a big car, which, with its folding seats in the middle, was able to hold ten people. I remember that we used to go fasting so that we might be able to receive Holy Communion, and we would take along our lunch in the trunk of the car so as to enjoy a meal after Mass. One day the car had a flat tire close to the town of Yauco while we were en route to Hormigueros. As the tire was being changed, we were almost hypnotized by the smell of rice and chicken. We did not receive Communion that day.

One person from my school whom I remember with great affection was Mother Vicente, who taught poor children in a place near our school which we affectionately called "the little school." Mother Vicente used to take me to the little school where I assisted her with catechism lessons. There I saw the needs of the poor and felt very sad because I did not know how to help them. I recall that on Holy Thursdays the sisters would invite the elderly to dinner and we, the pupils, would help serve them.

I must have been about nine years old when a promotional leaflet about a mission in India fell into my hands. I was very moved by the extreme poverty of the people of that country and decided to write to the mission and ask that they accept me as a missionary. They answered me very kindly, suggesting I wait until I was older before offering myself as a missionary; they also sent me more information, probably to keep alive the flame that had been ignited within me. My mother, with her customary wisdom, was very understanding and procured a flag of India which she placed in my room. She also bought a map of the world on which she circled India in red before hanging it on the wall of my room. On the other hand, she did not hesitate to show me the other side of the coin: parties, comfortable circumstances, and all those things that attract us human beings.

Between the ages of ten and thirteen, the idea of sacrifice became for me something very serious and useful. My brothers appeared to be more liberal and skeptical with respect to their faith and ideas, and in our discussions, I found I could not bring them around to my way of thinking. In an effort to bring about their "conversion," I decided to walk around with pebbles in my shoes (which I suppose contributed to the troubles I have had with my feet). I opted to eat what I did not like, to pray the rosary with my arms extended in the form of a cross, and to behave in a spirit of joy and service toward others; all this so that my brothers might be saved!

Apart from my concerns about my brothers' lack of faith, the rest of my life was sheer joy. Among ourselves we formed two clearly distinct groups: the older ones, Joe, Luis, and Saro; and the younger ones, Carlos, Herman, and me. Carlos, who was in the middle, served as a link between both groups. He was so good that when it came time to go to confession, he could not remember having done anything wrong and would instead confess the faults of his brothers and sisters: "My brother Joe, hit me...Saro made faces at me..." and on it went. The older ones would assume the role of bosses whenever our mother had to go away for a time to our country home in Adjuntas because of her ill health.

Those were difficult days for us younger ones since the older ones had exaggerated notions of their role, especially the boys. Saro tended to act in a maternal manner in my regard. She was a romantic and a dreamer and, being nine years my senior, would take it upon herself to educate me to be a refined young lady. One of Saro's special qualities was that she was very creative. I was quite impressionable, and one day while I was bathing, she pointed out an ant that was climbing up the tiles of the bathroom. Suddenly an effective and subtle way of controlling me occurred to her. She approached the ant and put her ear up to it, as if the insect were speaking to her; then she began to whisper things to the ant. Needless to say, I was awed and filled with curiosity. When I asked her what the ant was saying, she began a fairy tale that was to last for years. First she told me that this was the queen of the ants, and that during the night she would recover her true identity and would go off to visit her kingdom. When she arrived there, the ants would inform her of all the faults I might have committed during the day and what attitudes she would need to correct in me. Each day brought a new story, another enchanting and magical recital. It was in this special manner that my dear Saro taught me how to become a disciplined child.

My brother Luis was stricter. One day while we were waiting for dinner, I noticed that my brother Joe was munching on a small piece of fried cod fish, my favorite dish, so I proceeded to do likewise. As a punishment, Luis ordered me to my room without supper. After everyone had left, the cook, who was very fond of me, came to my room with something to eat, and later in the evening Luis went out for a walk and returned with some ice cream to console me. On the other hand, Luis was intrepid and possessed of a scientific mind. Once a parachutist came to Ponce. Luis was deeply impressed and, being neither stupid nor lazy, he climbed to the roof of our house on León Street, opened an umbrella, and leapt to the street. By the grace of God he did not hurt himself seriously, but I'm sure he did not soon forget that leap. On another occasion, he invented a homemade telegraph system that actually worked; it was so effective that the police showed up at our house wanting to investigate whether some sort of spy was intercepting government communications since we were at that time in the midst of the First World War.

Joe was always the most liberal one in the family; he was never in accord with those conservative individuals charged with monitoring our behavior. When Mother would pick up the strap to punish him for one of his infractions of discipline, he would run away in terror shouting: "Help, help, they're going to kill me," even before my mother had laid a finger on him. I remember that he used to argue with his teacher, Stella Márquez, about accents over certain letters in words, saying that they were idiotic since no one would be so stupid as to say *"azucár"* just because the word did not have an accent. He led a rather bohemian existence and his friends were the artists of that era. He was the first in our family to collect Puerto Rican paintings. He was truly an extraordinarily generous person.

My brother Herman was the only one who was unable to impose his will upon me. He was always in a hurry and charged with taking me to school and to Mass, while trying always to get me to do what he wanted. I would rebel, and so we rarely enjoyed a peaceful day.

While I was still in elementary school, my mother became ill and was no longer able to watch over me. I was paying more attention to my bicycle than I was to my books. At my sixth grade graduation I received no honors, flowers, medals or gifts; it was the logical result of my lack of interest in my studies. I recall that at my eighth grade graduation the exercises were held on the second floor of the school, and ended with a triumphal procession down the stairs where our relatives were waiting for us. My mother could not be present because of her illness, but at the foot of the stairs stood my sister-in-law, Dorothy Allers, my brother Joe's wife, an American who had graduated from Goucher College in Baltimore and was a member of the honor society, Phi Beta Kappa. I felt sad and embarrassed at seeing her shocked and disappointed expression at seeing me come down without a single award. But she recovered quickly, and without further ado, exclaimed: "This girl does not know how to study; she must be taught." Thus it was that with her help I learned to read English. I began by reading Peter Pan and later started to explore the world of English literature. Thus it was that my laziness regarding study became a thing of the past. I was then twelve years old.

I graduated from high school with high honors. The world of the intellect had begun to fascinate me when in 1928 the hurricane, San Felipe, hit the island. A period of severe economic depression followed. My four brothers were already studying in the United States, and that in itself was sufficient economic pressure for my father. He could not take them away from their studies so that I might continue mine. His words were: "Men without a profession are nothing; but you can marry a good professional and dedicate yourself to your home just as your mother and sister have done. The best place for a woman is in the home, looking after her husband and educating her children." My mother had a different opinion; she said to me: "If you want to be a worthy companion of a professional, or want to live independently, you must study."

My only option at the time was the University of Puerto Rico in Río Piedras where it was said that one would lose one's faith, something I was not prepared to risk. I found myself at a crossroads. On the one hand, I did not want to lose my faith, nor did the Religious of the Sacred Heart want that for me; like my father, they would rather have seen me become a simple housewife. On the other hand, my own intellect seemed to ask more of me, my common sense was telling me that my mother was right about the importance of studying, and I felt that I could deal with whatever situations I might have to face in Río Piedras. Thus, at sixteen years of age I began university studies while living at the boarding school of Trinity Academy run by the Missionary Servants of the Most Holy Trinity. This was, in my opinion, the ultimate guarantee that my faith would be preserved.

Actually, I arrived at the university with great hopes. When I began to taste university life with its activities, sports, and parties, I was totally fascinated. I recall making many new friends of both sexes during that first semester. One of those friends, a young man with whom I got along extremely well and had much in common, presented me with a copy of the book, *Platero y yo* by Juan Ramón Jiménez, but my classmates teased me by saying that he had given me a book about a donkey. We used to go out to have a good time in groups and enjoyed ourselves immensely. At the same time—and something not unusual for me—I pursued my apostolate among the poor that the Missionary Servants had entrusted to me. I became a member of their Apostolic Missionary Cenacle, and would accompany the sisters on their visits to the poor communities of Río Piedras and Caimito; we tried to assist the people in every way we could, and I taught catechism to the children.

Thus did the months pass, and the last day of final exams

of my first semester came. I was seventeen. Suddenly I sensed a strange foreboding and felt I did not want to remain in Río Piedras. At the last minute I joined some friends and took what we called a *"carro público"*—a car which traveled from one town to another, and in which one could rent a seat—to go to Ponce. I had to sit on the floor because I had not reserved a seat. When I arrived home, my sister and her children were there; my mother was seriously ill. At first I could not understand my sister's anxiety, since my mother's condition did not appear to be very grave. Far from complaining, she talked to me about a dress she was making for me for Christmas. At dawn of the following day, our relative, Father Noel, who lived in the Playa, came to our house. We all gathered around my mother's bed with the exception of my brother Luis who was away from the island at the time. It was nine o'clock when Luis arrived, and upon seeing him, Mother exclaimed: "I'm so glad you've come, my son!" Those were her last words and she closed her eyes for the last time.

Following my mother's death, I gave myself totally to my studies and apostolate as well as to the other activities I had been pursuing at the university. These months of extreme effort and activity finally took their toll on my health. A type of anemia took hold of my body and the doctor prescribed, among other things, a year of rest. I asked the doctor when I should begin, and he answered: "Enjoy the week-end and begin on Monday," to which I responded "If I must do it, I shall begin right now." I took a leave from the university, gathered up my belongings, and left for my home in Ponce. There I seemed to grow worse, and my father sent me to our country home in Adjuntas.

While I was convalescing in the country, Father Thomas Augustine Judge, founder of the Congregation of the Missionary Servants of the Blessed Trinity, came for a visit to Puerto Rico and heard about me. I imagine he must have been told about my interest in helping the poor, and so he wanted to meet me and made the trip to Adjuntas. The day he arrived he was deeply impressed by the beauty of the countryside and spent the day strolling around the grounds of our estate with my father and getting to know the flowers and fruits that grew there. (I recall that later he wrote about them). I was lying down when he arrived and saw him from my window. He looked like a man of great holiness and quiet authority. After dinner he indicated that he wished to give me a special blessing. It was the blessing of the Most Holy Trinity, which he reserved for important moments. If I remember correctly, he prayed for approximately ten minutes. His final words were: "Daughter, get well, God needs you to help so many poor children here in Puerto Rico." Later, after the priest left, my sister-in-law Lorencita (who spoke and understood English very well), said to my father: "Look, I think he has convinced her that she should be a nun."

With that hope, I began to give some thought to my mission in life and in Puerto Rico. These reflections served as a stimulus that helped me regain my health. About a month after that visit, I was able to leave my bed. I sensed something very special; I felt as if a star in the firmament of my life, the star that illumined my vocation, was growing brighter, and shedding light on the path I was to take. I returned to Ponce to care for my brothers and my widowed father, but also to respond to the call of my vocation by means of my apostolate among the poor. I also renewed my social and sports activities. I continued making retreats in the house in which I had lived in Río Piedras, and Father Judge would write, giving me spiritual direction.

On one of those retreats, I told Father Judge about my uneasiness regarding the religious life; my father had interpreted my desire to become a nun as an escape from reality, an escape I was seeking because of the absence of my mother. I also spoke to Fr. Judge about my longing to be faithful to the Lord during the years of my youth. He suggested that I wait until I was twenty-one to enter the convent and that, meanwhile, I should obey my father in everything. With respect to my fidelity, he indicated that I could make what I would now call a "pre-vow" of chastity. I thought that was a marvelous idea and, on my knees, said a simple prayer he had given me. After that I experienced great strength and renewed devotion in giving all my love to Jesus.

I began by imitating the example my mother had set in her service on behalf of the poor. If anyone came to our home and I saw there might be a need, I would ask what that need might be and how I could be of assistance. I likewise continued cultivating my relationships with my family, visiting my sister Saro in Humacao and my dearest brother-in-law, Adalberto Roig, whom I have always considered as a very special brother. I also pursued my social activities, especially the outdoor ones, such as horseback riding, swimming, tennis, and attending parties and dances.

I was familiar with the work of the Apostolic Missionary Cenacle that I had come to know during my semester at the University in Río Piedras; I still had classmates at the house where I had resided during my studies in Río Piedras who had just graduated from the University of Puerto Rico. I thought it a good idea to form a group in Ponce, since these classmates were returning home at that time. Before we realized it, we had formed (in 1932) the first lay missionary group in Ponce. Among those who became part of that initial group were the sisters, Falina, Mabel, and Carmen Rivera, Frances Crooke, Josefina Villamarzo, and several others. We were joined by my childhood friend, Olga

Schuck who, although not a part of the Río Piedras group, had a great desire to share our apostolate.

One great blessing was that the majority of the young women in the group shared the spirit and charism of Father Judge. Each person would select her mission and work at it; afterwards we would meet as a group to share our experiences and difficulties and inform one another about the work realized. We would help one another and, at times, do a specific work together. I remember a certain occasion when a few of us were walking by the Central Mercedita sugar factory looking for a place where we might be permitted to give catechism lessons. We stopped at a house and asked the owner if she knew of a place. She told us we could use the yard of her house, but warned us that we had to be quiet because the gentleman of the house was ill with throat cancer and could not bear to hear noise. Actually, the gentleman spent most of his time cursing and was usually in a very foul mood. But we did nothing to destroy the "harmony" that existed in the house. We used the yard, and the only things that could be heard were the recitation of the catechism and the songs of the children. Some time later my friends and I were walking along the Mercedita area on a Sunday and, providentially, I thought of that poor sick man and suggested to my friends that we visit him. When we arrived, we found him in his last agony and, by means of signs since he could not speak, he asked us to call a priest. Thankfully, the priest came in time and the man died in peace.

Each day I felt more and more the call of my Beloved in my heart. On one occasion I communicated to a priest this ardent desire to give myself to the Lord, and I told him about the problem of my father's negative attitude. The priest, in good faith, suggested that I escape to the Cenacle of the Missionary Servants. After reflecting upon his words for a while, I remembered the words of Father Judge, who had died by that time, that I obey my father in everything and that I enter the convent at twenty-one. That recollection persuaded me that Father Judge would not have approved of the action I was contemplating; I regained my peace, turned away from the idea of escape, and decided to wait.

In the year 1934 I was teaching catechism on the street named "25 de enero." I remember writing a story inspired by a very special child named Luz María, which appeared in a small periodical called *Holy Ghost Magazine* published in Philadelphia. Luz María was a twelve year old girl; she was hunch-backed and lived on that street with her mother and step-father, who clearly neglected her. She was sweet and generous and, having made her First Communion, was truly my right hand in teaching catechism. One day she felt a searing pain in her chest. Since her family ignored her distress, she walked alone, slowly and with great difficulty, to Tricoche Hospital to get help. When she got there, she was told to go home as there was nothing wrong with her. She began the painful walk home and, upon arriving there, collapsed and died. She had died of asphyxiation and remained there on the floor until I arrived. I found her covered with flies and asked her family what they planned to do. They answered that they did not know what they would do since they were penniless. I covered her body with a sheet and ran off to get help. I spoke with my friends and we procured the services of a funeral director who came with a coffin and car to transport her to her final resting place. Luz María's life had been extinguished, but the star of my vocation to serve the poorest of the poor began to shine even more brightly.

Besides teaching catechism and engaging in apostolic works, I would get up early on Sundays to attend Mass at the Church of Santa Teresita in a poor neighborhood of

Ponce. I would take my brother Joe's car (he used to lend it to me without asking any questions), and I would ride around the neighborhoods, teaching catechism and rounding up children to take to Mass. At first there were just five or six, but each Sunday there were more and more until they no longer fit in the car and would sit on the trunk or stand on the running board on either side of the vehicle. One morning I awakened with chicken pox and was upset because the children would have no one to take them to Mass. Then Joe and Florence (his second wife), offered to pick up the children and drive them to Mass. I told them where they could pick up the first children who would then give them directions for picking up the rest. That day on his return, Joe said: "Now I understand why each Monday morning the car is in such bad shape!"

Around that time we began to organize the town's shoeshine boys and newspaper vendors. We would meet and converse with them, procure clothes for them, and find locations where they could sell papers or shine shoes. My father was the owner of the building where the Habana cinema was located. Using my connections, I was able to create a distribution center there for candies and other tidbits, as well as free tickets for the movies. We would gather the young people and talk to them about God and how, in Him alone, would they find happiness. I felt like a real missionary. I remember one young man named Picón, who was the leader of the shoe-shine contingent, but who preferred to steal for a living than to engage in honest work. I gave him no peace until I was able to convince him that his actions were not right, and eventually he became my helper. In this way, and in many other ways, we were able to help countless young people.

My life was well balanced in every way, since I had time to do my apostolic work, which I tried to undertake responsibly and seriously with my friends. At the same time, I led a very active social life. I attended parties with my brothers Carlos, Joe, and his wife Florence. Every year I enjoyed the Carnival in San Juan and went on delightful picnics with my friends. I visited my beloved Saro and Adalberto in Humacao where I had another group of friends, among whom were Saro's nieces and nephews by marriage. I truly enjoyed the days of my youth. In addition, the Cenacle group and I planned the "Fiestas de Cruz"—folk celebrations held every May in honor of the Holy Cross. My friends and sports companions cooperated generously with their economic support for our numerous projects.

Thus, between experiences of stark reality and other, more pleasant events, four years finally passed. Four years of silent waiting for the final and definitive surrender of myself to the One who said: *"before I formed you in the womb, I knew you, and before you were born I consecrated you"* (Jeremiah 1:5).

My twenty-first birthday was fast approaching. I began to fill out the necessary papers for my entrance into the convent. Although my father did not speak about it, he was still reluctant to see me become a nun, least of all with the Missionary Servants of the Most Blessed Trinity who worked solely with the poor. Since he suspected that this was precisely the path I was determined to take, he planned a trip to Cuba so that I might meet my aunt, Sister Isolina Ferré, a member of the Congregation of the Apostles of the Sacred Heart. We were in Cuba on July 22, the Feast of Saint Mary Magdalene. I went to Mass at the Academy of the Sacred Heart in Tejadillo where there were several Madames of the Sacred Heart, friends of mine from Ponce. They were hoping that I might decide to enter their congregation. For my part, I was confused because, while I felt called to the Missionary Servants, I wanted in my heart to please my father and the Madames for whom I had great affection.

That day our Heavenly Father expressed clearly his wishes for me in the Gospel read at that Mass. This is the passage that totally dissipated all doubt and anguish from my heart:

> "While Jesus was in Bethany at the house of Simon the leper, a woman carrying a jar of costly perfume came up to him at table and began to pour it on his head. When the disciples saw this, they grew indignant, protesting 'What is the point of this extravagance? This could have been sold for a good price and the money given to the poor.'...Jesus said to them 'The poor you will always have with you but you will not always have me.'" (Mt 26:6-11)

Once again the light of the star that illumined my vocation shone brightly at this crucial moment of my life. I began to realize that my family name and our social position could be converted into a jar of alabaster. I would voluntarily choose to break this jar so that what poured out would be an ointment that was the essence of my life, apart from name or fame, and might serve to anoint Him who would be the Lord of my life: Jesus. Everything became clear, and all doubts disappeared as I made the decisive choice: I would give my life to God in the Congregation of the Missionary Servants of the Most Holy Trinity. There I would not be Sister Isolina Ferré, but a sister with any name they might give me. I did not care, as long as I could serve God among the poorest of people.

When I returned from Cuba, I knew that as my birthday approached, things would become more difficult and I developed a strategy. I went to my brother Joe, who had always been objective and possessed of an open and liberal mind; I spoke to him about my father's attitude in not wanting me to be a nun. He told me not to worry, but to leave everything in his hands. What I did not know is that my father had also sought out an advocate, my brother Luis, who also assured him that he would take care of everything.

On September 5, 1935, my birthday, I arose early and went to the dining room where my father was having breakfast and reading the paper. I said to him: "Papa, I am twenty-one today. Now I am an adult and I want to enter the convent." His response was total silence. Then we each went off to meet with our respective advocates. Luis called me and tried to convince me that what I wanted to do I could just as easily accomplish through his company as a social worker among his employees. Joe went to Papa's office where an unforgettable exchange of words took place:

Joe: "Isolina wants to go away to study."

Papa: "No, she wants to go away to be a nun."

Joe: "No, she wants to go away to study to be a nun."

My father was a typical man of his times and, as such, considered it a weakness to change his mind. The word "study" was a plank he could grasp to save face, and thus not appear to fall into that much feared "weakness."

Papa: "Well, if it's to study, that's different; let her go."

Joe: "No, she can't just go; you must take her, just as you did with each of us when we went to study in the United States."

I remember packing my bags and going to say good-bye to the family. Before I left, my father gave me my mother's jewels, the inheritance she had left for me when she died. I decided to give some to each of my siblings and take the rest so I could donate them to the Congregation I was about to join. I shall never forget my nieces and nephews. Alcito, Saro's son, hid my hat in an effort to prevent my leaving. When we finally found it, he said to me:

"Auntie Iso, I don't want you to go."

My father and I boarded the ship, the "Coamo"; on board I met many friends who were going to the United States to study in prestigious universities. During the voyage, in our conversations, they asked me where I was going to study. Knowing what it was costing my father to accept the path I had chosen, so different from theirs, I said: "I'm going to a very special university in Philadelphia." They marvelled at that, and my father was profoundly grateful. Thus it was that, step by step, the star that illumined the path of my life brought me to the realization of the Lord's call to serve Him in my brothers and sisters, the very poor. Father Thomas Augustine Judge, with his experience and spirituality, could sense that much better than I, and on one occasion had written me the following:

> The theme of the wonderful design for your life is becoming apparent. It is beautiful. It leaves one in awe. I ask myself if even you can perceive it. Realize that there is a special providence working in your life. You can now begin to follow the design of the Divine Artist's hand.

The Novitiate

This is a blessed year for six Missionary Servants of the Most Blessed Trinity: the year of their Golden Jubilee of Service to the Triune God.

It was 1935 when these six women found themselves for the first time in Philadelphia at the Mother House. Sisters Mary Tonra and Agnes John Donlon came from Brooklyn. Sister Jean Anthony from New York State. Sister María Cristina González from Aguada, Milagros Marie Ortíz from Coamo and Sister Isolina from Ponce. There they began six months of postulancy and a year of noviceship; and from that moment the flame was ignited that to this day burns in our hearts. That light has been a reflection of the Light who is the Lord who drew us to the Religious life, but it also sealed us, marked us so that we might be light to that part of the world where we were to live our mission.

"For all things were made by Him and nothing was made without Him. What He made was life; the life that is light for all men."

During these 50 years we have met several times—and I believe that each has been light for those around her...

And now? Now we are in the Providential Hands of our Triune God who will determine the dark places into which we must shed light—and He too, when the hour comes, will receive the dying flame of our dedication.

It shall be as the Psalmist declared: "And they shall shine as stars in the firmament."

—Editorial from *El Playero,* no. 71, April-June 1985, p. 3.

*O*n September 23, 1935, my father and I arrived in Philadelphia, known as the city of brotherly love. We were met at the station by Sister Marie of the Precious Blood. I was glad to see a Trinitarian sister, but I was a little scared when I saw that she was the driver of the car, for she was tiny, not even five feet tall, and had something wrong with her leg that made her limp when she walked. I was reassured as soon as she took the steering wheel and realized she was a magnificent driver. First impressions do not always tell you the truth about persons or things.

That first trip with Sister Marie to the motherhouse initiated my learning about the new culture into which I was to be integrated; it began with something as trivial as a "hamburger." En route, I observed with curiosity some small white houses with signs that read "White Castle" and I asked, in all innocence: "Sister, what does that 'White Castle' mean?"

Smiling, she answered: "That's where people buy hamburgers when they're hungry."

I was surprised, and I said: "But why so many White Castles? Are there that many people who eat hamburgers?"

She answered: "All the time; it's a great favorite."

Then I said: "Ah, they must be like our little *bacalâitos fritos.* Father smiled in the midst of his sadness.

After a long while, I saw in the distance what I perceived to be "The House with Seven Towers" about which I used to read in fairy tales as a child. It was such a beautiful building! It seemed old, made of grey stone and with many towers that rose heavenward. I was enchanted, but my surprise was even greater when I discovered that it was the motherhouse and novitiate. The general custodian at the time, Mother Marie of the Incarnate Word, was waiting for us. She was a lady of such great sweetness and deep spirituality, and possessed of such a great heart, that right then and there I felt a bond of affection that was never to be broken. Later we met the other sisters, including, Sister Mary Francis who was the general assistant and the novice mistress.

Shortly after, some families from New York arrived with their daughters who were to form part of my group. They were Sister Mary Fidelis Tonra, Sister Agnes John Donlon, and two Puerto Ricans who had arrived before, Sister Milagros Marie Ortíz from Coamo and Sister María Cristina González from Aguada. Upon meeting them all, I felt a lot better, although Father seemed to feel out of place among so many nuns, and sad at having to leave me at such a great distance from home.

I was invited to go to change clothes and put on the uniform or habit (I hardly know what to call it) that would distinguish us as postulants, different from the other sisters. Father was at my side, and I recalled at that moment that my brother Joe and I had told him that I was going away to study. Suddenly, I felt the same compassion for my father that I had felt when we were aboard the "Coamo"; I decided to postpone putting on the habit until after he had left. Finally, Father and I separated with the hope that we would meet again soon.

After my father left I was taken to the chapel. Upon entering, I knelt, and immediately felt the kind of relief one experiences when finally achieving what one has struggled so many years to attain. I noticed on the wall a painting of the annunciation, in which the angel is announcing to Mary that she has been chosen by the Spirit from among all women. At that moment, Mary's response to the angel echoed in the very core of my being: "Be it done unto me according to thy word." I felt that Mary was in solidarity with me, since at the moment in which each of us had verbalized our "yes" to the Lord, neither she nor I could have imagined what awaited us; we knew only Who it was to whom we had entrusted ourselves. I say this, not in any way to compare myself with Mary, but simply to note that her "yes" gave me the courage to say mine. I realized then that I was entering into a new and different world, an unknown world, with different cultures, different people, prayers in English...Nevertheless, I felt confident that in the midst of the unknown, the Lord's light would illumine my path and give me the necessary strength to begin my new life. We had Benediction of the Blessed Sacrament in that humble chapel which was small, but lovely and warm. That blessing confirmed that my life was totally His, and thus began my life as a Missionary Servant of the Most Blessed Holy Trinity.

Later, we went to put on our new attire as postulants. I was truly happy that my father had not remained to see me walking by in that dress, and this for two reasons. First, because it was not new, and second, because it was horribly large and had to be held in place with a cord around my waist. When we looked at one another, we burst out laughing. Mine was the most comical outfit, since I looked like a broom tied in the middle. My postulancy had begun. I bade farewell to that other world to which, until then, I had belonged, and began with great expectations the new life in which my Lord had asked that I accompany Him so as to form me as a missionary for his cause.

Much to my surprise, I felt no sadness during those first few days; I was so happy to be living those moments, so intense and so important to me, that I did not, for a moment, experience the separation from my family. But two days later, while at breakfast, the memory of my family came strongly to mind. As I recount it today, it makes me laugh, but while I was living through it, my pain was intense. We were seated at table in silence, as we were not allowed to speak. While we were having breakfast, someone was reading aloud in English the life of a saint; I tried to listen. At the same time, I was trying to eat a breakfast to which I was not accustomed, forcing myself to believe that what I was doing was good. Suddenly, the face of my brother Carlos and my other brothers and sister came vividly to mind. It seemed to me that I could almost see them laughing as they observed my struggles with that hard bread that I could hardly bite into. The crisis came when, to my surprise, I asked myself: "My God, what am I doing here?" Tears began to flow uncontrollably down my cheeks, and I started to realize that the sacrifice had begun.

Finally, that interminable breakfast came to an end and I went up to my room. I did not realize that the Novice Mistress had been aware of my distress. While I was making my bed, she came into the room and said: "You seem sad."

I answered: "Yes, I was missing my brothers and sisters."

And then, very wisely, she pointed out the following to me: "Now is your moment to know how to listen to the Lord's call, and to pronounce your "yes" profoundly and consciously. Remember that you are not, nor ever will be, alone; and that they (your siblings) are, and always will be, in your heart and in your prayers."

I soon recovered and reintegrated myself into that process, so necessary in confirming my unconditional surrender to the Lord. With feet firmly fixed in my present reality, I determined to submit myself to the religious formation for which I had come. My usual joy returned, and I became friends with everyone. I was the only Puerto Rican who spoke fairly good English, and so I helped my two compatriots become an integral part of our group.

Life in the novitiate consisted of much prayer, formation and work. The latter pleased me very much because at home, although I had been assigned certain tasks, it was not the same. Here I had to undertake every kind of domestic work, most of which I had never done before. I had to wash

41

dishes, clean and scrub floors, and do other such tasks. How I enjoyed those jobs! Although it may seem somewhat unreal, when I finished my duties, I used to ask my companions to let me do part of theirs. I was very happy there.

The months passed and my first winter arrived, bringing with it my first snowfall. I was thrilled with that marvelous spectacle, the snow falling so softly and transforming the natural world into one that was sublimely white. My American companions were given permission to play out in the snow, but we Puerto Ricans had to remain indoors, since this was our first winter and it seemed prudent to protect us from the cold. I watched from the window how my companions were enjoying themselves, and showed on my face the delight I was feeling for them, even though I could not join them. The general custodian, who was a very observant and maternal lady, called me and said: "Look, why don't you wrap yourself warmly in a coat and go out to play with the others." Hardly had she uttered those words, when I was plunging into the snowbanks. I shall never forget those moments. I enjoyed myself immensely, even when they gave us shovels to clear the doorways. I was having such a good time that I did not even feel the cold. Later, after we had finished our recreation time, we came indoors only to find waiting for us delicious cups of hot chocolate that the general custodian had prepared to warm us. That day we really felt the warmth of a true home. We were all young, and the sister custodian had allowed us to go out and play in the snow and, afterwards, had received us with wonderful chocolate. It was just like home. Above all, we had learned a lesson in humility and the meaning of real service to one's neighbor from our dear general custodian. This helped me to understand that my home could be anywhere in the world where I was doing God's Will.

I enjoyed that winter immensely, especially since I

learned to go sleigh riding. The novitiate was located on a small hill, and so we were able to climb to the top and slide down speedily. Again and again we had great fun running up and down with sleds. We did not realize that in riding down that hill we were also destroying the little snow-covered saplings that one of the older nuns had taken so much trouble to plant before the winter. I recall that when the spring came and the nun discovered the disaster, she exclaimed: "Something very bad has crushed these little trees I planted. Only half of them remain; it must have been a small animal." Little did she know that the "small animal" had been the postulants who had completely taken over the entire field during the winter. Somehow it must have been discovered later, because the following winter that area was out of bounds to us. Thanks to those precautions, the motherhouse today is surrounded by beautiful and robust trees.

At the end of six months of postulancy, we had to submit three names to the novice mistress from which she would choose one by which we would henceforth be called. Once again I renounced the opportunity to select a name to my liking and left the decision in the hands of the general custodian. Normally, symbolic or biblical names would be chosen. During the ceremony, the Rule book was placed in my hands and I remember hearing with some shock: "María Isolina Ferré, henceforth you will be known as Sister Thomas Marie." After the initial surprise, I understood that the name was given to me in memory of our Father founder who had helped me discern my call to work with the abandoned and marginalized. Marie was given to me in memory of my mother whose name was Mary.

The formation we received in the novitiate was designed to prepare us in such a way that when the time came to pronounce our vows of chastity, obedience, and poverty, we might do so with full awareness of our commitment. For some reason, I took obedience very literally. I said yes to everything without asking any questions or expressing any doubts. Two incidents will demonstrate this. I was very thin, perhaps because food was not in great abundance and the work was quite rigorous. One day I was standing at the exit door when my mistress of novices was leaving to see the doctor. As she passed me, she put her hand in the pocket of her habit, took out five coins, and gave them to me saying: "Here, go and fatten up." Then she left.

I thought: "How can I get fat on five cents?" But, since I was extraordinarily obedient, I crossed the street to a small store and said to the clerk: "I have to gain some weight with this money." He sent me off with a small bag of jelly beans. Upon my return, all my companions wanted one and I would not give them any, saying: "Sorry, but I'm the one who has to get fat by order of the novice mistress."

Later, when they told her the story, she said: "One has to be very careful with that Sister Thomas, because she carries obedience so far that one never knows what might happen."

On another occasion, I went to her office and said: "My shoes need repairing; they have holes in the soles."

She answered: "Take them to the shoemaker."

I said: "But, they're the only ones I have."

She insisted: "Take them to the shoemaker." At that moment she was very preoccupied and I don't think she was paying much attention to me.

I was on my way out, when suddenly she seemed to recall my attitude toward obedience and came after me saying: "Come here, you're liable to go to the shoemaker, leave your shoes, and come back barefooted."

I said: "Well, I don't have any other shoes."

Thus it was that they always had to be very careful with the orders they gave me, since I apparently lacked any sense of limit or prudence in carrying them out, however absurd they might seem.

I ate a great deal, but could not gain weight. On another occasion, as Thanksgiving Day was approaching, Sister Peter, who was elderly and in charge of begging for alms and food for the congregation, asked the general custodian that I be allowed to accompany her on her rounds. Sister Peter used to walk or take the trolley, but since I knew how to drive and had a license, she asked that I be given permission to take the car. The general custodian assented and, half in jest, said: "Take Sister Thomas, but remember that you have to feed her because she likes to eat."

We set out and Sister was delighted because we had the car. The day turned out to be a tragicomedy because Sister was not familiar with traffic regulations and I stubbornly did whatever I was told, so we violated every sign and traffic light we encountered. She would say to me: "Go down this street because we have to get to that building." What she did not know was that to get to that building, we would have to enter through another street and not the one she indicated, which was a one-way street. We found ourselves facing oncoming traffic and angry drivers leaning on their horns and shouting unprintable words. She exclaimed: "Oh, my God, I have a weak heart, and I'm going to get worse if you continue to enter the wrong streets!"

I answered: "But didn't you tell me to go down that street?"

What a day! Fortunately, I was a good driver and we were able to dodge the cars that came at us. We arrived home with arms filled with apples, hams, turkeys and other foodstuffs, in spite of our numerous adventures.

With respect to my family, we kept in touch with some frequency. My father wrote regularly. I remember some letters in particular in which he was, in his own way, preparing me to give me certain news: he had fallen in love again. It seems that on the day he left me at the novitiate in Philadelphia, and while on the return voyage to Puerto Rico, he met Pepita Goenaga who had brought her son, Luis Sala, to the States to study. After a few months, and after having laid the groundwork, Father and she appeared at the novitiate. With her arm in my father's, she approached me with a bouquet of flowers. Although I had anticipated that meeting, the situation somehow confused me. I blushed a little, and at the moment of introducing them to my companions, the words that came out were: "My father and...my mother-in-law." My nervousness made me unaware of what I had said, but the laughter of my companions took care of letting me know. Thereafter, for a long time the novitiate joke was: "Sister Thomas and her mother-in-law."

Another day my sister Saro announced she was coming to visit me. What a tremendous fuss resulted when the general custodian asked to see my hands, and saw how red, cut, and cracked they were. She was horrified, since my scrubbing of floors, peeling apples and potatoes (which generally resulted in small cuts) and other such chores had left my hands in a very different condition from Saro's, who never had to do such tasks. Besides, I used to bathe the dogs and work in the garden. Grimy, rough, and cut was how my hands looked. I was given creams and other remedies to whiten and soften them, but they did no good. When Saro came, I decided to put my hand inside my habit sleeves, but in greeting her, I let them show, and Saro was shocked.

There is one story I remember with great affection and which imparted to me a sense of human warmth. At one time I found a dog and was permitted to keep it. It was a marvelous thing for me, since I had always been accustomed to having my little pets at home. His name was Laddie and he was black with large, droopy ears. I was warned: "If you want to keep the dog, you must take care of it and feed it." Since we were a poor congregation, we had scarcely any leftover food after meals. I took to saving bottles wherever I could find them and exchange them for dog food. My companions used to comment: "That's a real sacrifice; it's not easy to go around picking up bottles to get food for that dog." Actually, I have always loved animals and was happy to do it. Laddie used to accompany us everywhere, even to class and chapel. Even the novice mistress, who loved him very much, would go down to the cellar where he used to sleep, to be sure he was all right and arrange his bed. One winter he became ill and we took care of him as best we could but, at the time, we could not afford to take him to a veterinarian. One evening, while we were praying in chapel, one of the sisters signaled to me to look toward the door. There was Laddie, looking very sad, as if he were there to say his final prayers. I took him back to the cellar, put mentholatum on him and returned to the chapel. Later, before retiring, the novice mistress and I went down to see how he was. To our surprise, we found him dead. Then Sister Mary Francis said to me: "We have to take him outside; it's too hot down here to leave him." We looked around to see if we could find something in which to wrap him. Nearby we saw something that looked like a piece of awning material and wrapped him in it, placing him out on the snowy ground where the maintenance man could get him in the morning and bury him. Imagine our surprise when, the next morning, we saw the man coming toward us with a very angry look on his face. It seems we had wrapped the dog in his raincoat. I don't think he ever forgave us.

My novitiate days were truly filled with valuable lessons, many good times, and others not so good. It was such an intense experience that I was not aware of the passage of time until the day when I was called to be notified that the time had come to make my vows of poverty, chastity, and obedience to the Lord, and be prepared to serve and work as a Missionary Servant of the Most Blessed Trinity.

Sister Isolina in a jeep gathering the children for catechism through the mountains of Cabo Rojo.

View of La Playa streets when Sister Isolina first arrived in 1935.

One of the poor shacks in La Playa.

In Quest of a Vision

The first sewing workshop in the old garage of the convent in La Playa where we taught the women how to sew.

The despondency of the people in La Playa when Sister Isolina first arrived there.

Coronation of the Blessed Mother by the fishermen of La Playa, in a replica of the boat used by them for fishing (Yola).

1970: The beginning of the center which was called Centro de Orientacion y Servicios, located in the first floor of the cenacle.

One of the many families found in need of help in La Playa.

One of the many workshops for giving work and dignity to the young people of La Playa.

One of the first high school graduations from Centros Sor Isolina Ferré in 1978.

The fire that burned our first cenacle and offices in 1981.

The Missions

Our effort is not limited to a vain proclamation of personal holiness, like an empty echo of reality, but it must penetrate our daily living, making every action a concrete expression of our beliefs.

("*La paz armada*," article written by me and published in the paper, EL NUEVO DIA of Saturday, March 21, 1987.)

*M*y companions and I bade farewell to the novitiate in Philadelphia after being there a year and a half as postulants and novices. The parting was sad because we had become a very close family. However, the dream of finally embarking upon the very reason for our consecrated lives, which was the sowing of the seed of true hope in Jesus in the hearts of those who did not have it, encouraged us to forge ahead. Each of us was sent to a different mission, accompanied by experienced sisters who, in turn, would function as guides while we took our first steps as missionaries. Sister Anita was the sister assigned to me as companion and guide in this first mission.

NORTON, VIRGINIA (APRIL, 1937)

I was sent to Norton, Virginia, a mining town located in the Appalachian Mountains. It was a very poor place. The miners no longer had work and had scarcely any hope that things might some day change. We arrived there to teach catechism and to share in their struggle. We were assigned to a small parish in the town. The pastor was Belgian, and of a somewhat abrasive and inflexible disposition. We were lodged in a small house behind the rectory with the minimum of amenities. I recall that, upon entering the house, we found the place filthy and everything thrown about; the last word you could use to describe that house was "orderly." The mattresses on the two small beds were old, dirty, and full of holes. Our stipend was to be fifty dollars a month with which we were expected to buy food, clothing, and household supplies. That was how we began.

The priest, who came from a culture very different from that of America, had problems with us. Our work in itself was difficult, but he made it more so. He insisted that we grow our own food while, at the same time, we did housework, taught catechism, and visited parishioners. We had to drive up perilous mountain roads to take him to say Mass and visit people. I remember one occasion when someone who was Catholic died. There were not many of our faith in that town, and the priest was really at his best. He emphasized that everything had to go especially well because such occasions were rare, and we had to carry out everything perfectly. I was to toll the church bells, act as sacristan by preparing the altar, etc., and be the altar server with all the duties that implied, such as lighting the incense. Next, I was to climb to the choir loft where Sister Anita was playing the organ and do what I had never done in my life: sing the hymns appropriate to the occasion. When it was over, I couldn't help but laugh because I never would have believed that I was capable of doing all those things.

Not everything was burdensome; we had our satisfactions. I remember a young lady, whom I shall call Viola because after many years working among so many beautiful people like her, my memory fails me as to her real name. She was a Protestant and lived nearby. Eventually, we became good friends. She had a sister who suffered from diabetes, and who would accompany us whenever we went for a walk. On these walks I came to know the town quite well. Viola and I could easily relate to one another since we were both young, and I think that she was puzzled by the fact that I was willing to dedicate myself to what I was doing instead of enjoying myself like others our age. She had great ambition to succeed in life and wanted to study. Many years later I found out through one of our sisters who was in Norton that she had converted to Catholicism. She had gone on to study education, and after receiving her degree, returned to work among her people.

Although I found myself in such a remote place, nevertheless, the protective eye of my family found me even there. One day my brother Carlos came to visit me. The best I could offer him was two fried eggs and a cup of black, but rather weak, coffee. My beloved brother seemed to enjoy it as if it had been a banquet.

Our mission to Appalachia was not of long duration, for after six months we were assigned elsewhere. Our Father founder had been of the opinion that transculturation could corrupt the very foundation of one's Catholicism and serve to corrupt one's faith, making it a mixture of several religions in one. Since the United States was receiving immigrants both from Europe and Puerto Rico, it was thought that such a phenomenon might occur. It was necessary to assist and strengthen our Catholics in their faith, but first they had to be identified. This would be done by taking a census of Catholics living in the United States, and I was one of the sisters assigned to this important undertaking.

CENSUS (OCTOBER 1937–OCTOBER 1940)

We began the census in Brooklyn. I was sent to a large parish surrounded by many apartment buildings occupied by persons of different nationalities; Catholics, Protestants, and Jews all lived in the same buildings. My task was not easy, because it involved not merely identifying the Catholics, but trying to communicate with a mixture of nationalities. I had to know how to identify the characteristics of each group and find the best way of approaching them. I remember feeling somewhat bewildered by the complexity of the mission and asked my more experienced sisters how I might recognize the Irish, the Italians, the Greeks, and the Jews, among others. They told me: "Never ring the bell of an apartment where you see a last name that ends with 'berg,' 'stein,' or 'witz' because they are Jewish. But where you see an Irish name, ring the bell." I answered: "But how will I know the name is Irish?" At that point, the Sisters burst out laughing as they were almost all Irish. Later they said: "Don't worry, you'll recognize them by their accent." I asked no more questions and commended myself to God, since that business of accents did not seem very practical, given my historical circumstances. Thus it was that God inspired me, because it occurred to me that there was a better way of detecting persons so different from Americans and from myself: it was the sense of smell. I would ring the bell and when the door was opened, if I could smell corned beef and cabbage, I knew I was in Irish territory. The smell of goulash exuded from Polish homes. The seasonings of the Italians were very similar to those of the Puerto Ricans. That way I began to interact with all the Catholics of different cultures. The Italians were lively and a bit gossipy (rather like us Puerto Ricans) and very willing to tell us their life stories and unusual happenings, as well as those of their neighbors. The Irish were happy and friendly people, and had a lively and colorful folklore. It was a time of great personal enrichment for me.

For three years I led a nomadic existence, not having any

fixed abode while I traveled and did my census work in different locations: Long Island, New York City, Washington, D.C., Connecticut, Baltimore, among others. I would travel alone or with other sisters, and I lived with different congregations of religious in various convents in which I was welcomed. It was a period of economic recession. Food was scarce and I could not have been thinner. On one occasion I was accompanied by Sister Augustine who was very delicate, and as thin or thinner than I. As a result, a priest who had met us and was later announcing our arrival to his parishioners in anticipation of our visit, described us as women "of profound asceticism and sacrifice." As we visited each home, the parishioners were able to confirm the pastor's words with their own eyes; and thereafter, to our surprise, they welcomed us with biscuits and milkshakes when we visited them. On other occasions, we did not have such good luck because the meals offered us in some convents made us feel like crying instead of eating. One evening we received a call from the motherhouse and somehow we let the general custodian know about our situation. She authorized us to buy cheese and fruit to satisfy our hunger.

In 1939 I was notified by the motherhouse that the time had come to pronounce perpetual vows. I arrived a few days early to make a spiritual retreat that would prepare me for that long-awaited event. As I was washing my only habit, I realized that the poor thing was beyond repair. The traveling from state to state, from parish to parish, exchanging companions, but not habits, had rendered the garment threadbare after much use and many washings. Upon seeing it, one of my companions asked me: "Do you expect to take such an important step in these remains of a habit?" I answered her calmly: "It doesn't matter, the important thing is that I be ready to make my permanent commitment to Christ." Word spread about my urgent need for clothes.

One of the older sisters, Sister James, found out and called me to her room, offering to lend me one of her habits. Later, some of my companions could hardly believe it, because Sister James was a bit unfriendly and many did not get along well with her. Thus it was that, in a borrowed habit, I made my promise of eternal surrender to Jesus.

After making my profession of perpetual vows, I was given fifteen days to visit my family. What joy! After four years away from my country and my loved ones, I was given time to return to see them. Upon arriving in San Juan, I was faced with a bit of a dilemma. Our congregation had a rule stating that no Sister could travel alone in a car with a man. I had been met by a pilot with a commercial plane rented by my family to take me to Ponce. For a moment, I was confused and thought: "My God, what should I do?" My common sense prevailed, and I found a solution. The rule specifically indicated a car, but said nothing about an airplane, so I boarded the plane with utmost peace of mind. What an experience! From the plane I could enjoy the beautiful scenery of Puerto Rico with its colorful landscape and tiny houses. What an inspiration! However, while aboard the plane, I felt that in obedience I was obliged to recount the incident to my superior. As I gazed upon the countryside with its poor homes, I wondered how I might report what had happened without getting into trouble. As soon as I could after my arrival, I wrote to the general custodian in more or less the following terms:

> "Upon arriving in San Juan, I was met by a plane sent by my family which took me to Ponce. During the flight I was able to observe our beautiful countryside and the poor little houses of my people. Then I experienced great pain in my heart. Are they receiving the message of Jesus? Are the children being taught the catechism to prepare them for their First Holy Communion? Sister, how I would love to be the one to bring the Light of Christ to my people...."

The letter was much more effective than I had hoped, because, as is evident, it is with my people that I have labored for most of my life's journey.

I recall telling my family what I had done, and they commented: "Isolina, what ideas you get!" I lived those days with great intensity, enjoying every moment of the fifteen days with my family.

After returning to the motherhouse in Philadelphia, I set out soon again to continue my census work, but after a few months that assignment was completed. There would be no more dashing from state to state with suitcase in hand. In the fall of 1940 I was assigned to Wareham, Massachusetts.

WAREHAM, MASSACHUSETTS (NOVEMBER 1940– SEPTEMBER 1943)

I was glad to find myself finally in one fixed location, in one cenacle (our congregation calls each of our convents by that name), instead of leading a nomadic existence. The place where I was to live and work was in Cape Cod and it would be the first time that our congregation had a mission there. The church was a new building that had just been opened. It was painted white and was called Saint Patrick's. Our work consisted of teaching catechism, doing other parish work, and training the altar boys. We were also assigned the area around the cranberry fields where people of mixed African and Portuguese extraction, originally from the Cape Verde Islands, who were called "Bravas," resided. Although, of course, they spoke Portuguese, I was able to understand them, because of the similarity with Spanish, and we established very good communication. The people who lived on Cape Cod were white families, refined in their manners and in their dealings with others. They were good people who esteemed us highly, but they were very racist. There was no way they would allow themselves to be integrated with the Bravas. Their prejudice was extraordinary, for they believed that hard work was not something that dignified the human person, since, according to them, it was what people like the Bravas had to do. The latter worked for them. They felt that refined people ought never to do work requiring the use of their muscles, and when they saw us washing windows, they were quite scandalized.

Besides the Bravas, there were also white Portuguese, Irish, and native New Englanders. We came to know all these families, although we did not work with the latter as most of them were Protestant. What I remember with greatest affection is the young people. We established a series of clubs by means of which we guided the young people and we organized great parties and delightful outings. The best part of all this was that we were able to integrate the white and black youths. It was a very edifying experience, both for them and for us. I also recall with great affection two young women from Cape Cod. One was a teacher, and both belonged to rich families and had been educated in the best schools. While we were at that mission, they came to know us and followed our work very closely—so much so that both decided to enter our novitiate and today are religious of our congregation.

That experience in Cape Cod became a determining factor with respect to what I would be doing in the future, because up to that point I had always had to follow the orders of others wherever I had been. For the first time, I was directing others: the altar boys as well as the boy scouts and girl scouts. Although I was responsible to Sister Bernice, I had considerable freedom of action. Since I was young, I was assigned to the children and the teenagers, while she, as a native New Englander, dignified in manner and in her dealings with others, worked with the adults on the Cape. Sister Bernice was a most charming person; she had worked with Indians for several years in southern Mississippi. Sister Bernice used to say that those Indians were expressionless; from looking at them, one could never guess what they might be feeling. Poor Sister Bernice had acquired something of that trait, and it was very funny when she would recount a humorous anecdote because her facial expression was not in harmony with her words. She was somewhat impassive, seldom smiling. To watch her was like seeing one of her beloved Indians. On the other hand, my other companion was younger than I and very shy; and so, since my personality was cheerful and extroverted, I ended up as the natural leader.

At about that time we heard on the radio about the attack on Pearl Harbor and the declaration of war by the president of the United States, Franklin Delano Roosevelt. We spent some of the years of the Second World War trying to bring about more harmonious relations between the young and the adults, stressing those things they had in common. Three years went by when, in September of 1943, we were called to the motherhouse to make our annual retreat.

In those days, it was customary to receive written orders regarding our assignments at the end of the annual retreat. I was happy because the retreat had proved very helpful to me, and actually, I had no inkling that my mission would be changed, since I had barely begun to do all I wanted in the place where I was stationed. What was my surprise when, upon reading my mission letter, I saw that instead of saying on Cape Cod. I was to be sent somewhere else:

"Dear Sister Thomas Marie,
May the grace and peace of the Holy Spirit be with you forever!

61

After prayer and consultation, I have decided to send you to Long Island City.

This ministry is a sacred responsibility that you are accepting; and by means of the service you render to the people of that place and the Sisters of that Community, you shall be a witness of God dwelling in your midst.

My world seemed to collapse around me. I had no time to say good-bye, since the letter was given to me on Friday and I was to report Monday morning to my new mission. Even Sister Bernice raised an outcry and presented objections, saying: "How can you take Sister Thomas? She's the most active of us!" But it was no use; obedience meant that I must say "amen" to every commmand of superiors.

LONG ISLAND CITY, NY (SEPTEMBER 1943–OCTOBER 1946)

God works in mysterious ways. Although I arrived in Long Island City somewhat downcast, I soon realized I was needed there. I was assigned to Saint Rita's parish, located in a largely Italian sector that was not as clean as Cape Cod. It had an immense housing project whose residents were mostly Italians although there were some Puerto Ricans. I was welcomed by Sister Louise who was much older than I. She was an Italian, with a stern personality and difficult disposition. The other sister assigned to that mission was the exact opposite: young, tiny, and possessed of a gentle voice; she had a physical impediment in one leg and limped when she walked. I thought that her physical limitation would prevent her from keeping up with our usual busy pace, but I was mistaken because it turned out that she walked faster than I. She tried not to impose on anyone and to be as self-sufficient as possible. She generally succeeded. I noticed on one occasion that, when she tried to cut her toe nails, she had to twist her body wildly before she could reach a single toe. From that moment on, I cut them for her. The incident brought back memories. I remembered the man who had no legs and whom my mother had helped to become self-sufficient; I recalled also my little hunchbacked friend and helper Luz María, who had died for lack of attention, and the sister who received me the day I entered the novitiate. Thus, I began to develop a profound awareness of the difficulties that persons with physical disabilities have to contend with.

Finally, we were given our major assignment: we were to teach catechism to groups of three hundred public school boys and girls in the sixth and seventh grades. I shall never forget that first day. We had to pick them up after school. I thought to myself: "After a whole day of classes, who would want to go to catechism school?" Certainly not children of that age! But that was the situation, and we had to cope with it. Sister Louise's task was to bring them to order with the help of her thunderous voice. We proceeded to the church and, without any introductions, I found myself facing three hundred adolescents who stared at me as if asking: "Now what?" I was paralyzed as thousands of thoughts raced through my mind: "My God, how am I going to control them? They're tired and don't want to be here; besides, I'm not the yelling type." Then the light came, and my fear and insecurity disappeared: "I'll tell them a story that will keep them busy the entire hour I have to spend with them."

Since I had to start with the rosary, and October was about to begin, I made up the following story: "Do you know what holiday we shall be celebrating in October? Columbus Day." They looked at one another as if saying, "So what?" I continued: "I must tell you what happened to Columbus. It seems that he had convinced some sailors that there was land on the other side of the ocean, and so they sailed away on three ships." I went to the blackboard and sketched the ships with sailors on board and continued: "After many weeks of sailing, they could see no land at all, so the sailors became desperate and infuriated. They wanted to kill Columbus and then return to Spain. Columbus was so frightened that his brain went on overtime and he had a brilliant idea. Would you like to know what it was?" Now interested, the children shouted: "Yes, yes, go on, tell us." "Columbus said to them: 'Listen, all of you, we'll make a deal: I'm going to say the rosary and if, by the time I finish, we have not sighted land, we shall return to Spain.' He began: 'In the name of the Father and of the Son and of the Holy Spirit...,' and he began to walk from stem to stern with his rosary in his hand. 'Hail, Mary, full of grace....' The sailors were moved and joined in the prayers....'Holy Mary, Mother of God....'" The children too joined in..."pray for us sinners...." I continued the story while at the same time thinking: "O God, make this hour pass by quickly!" "And so Columbus continued to pray, but the sailors were getting more and more impatient, until when he was just finishing the Hail Holy Queen, and the sailors were ready to pounce on him, suddenly a cry was heard: 'Land, land!' and Columbus was saved, and America was discovered." They did not realize that I too had been saved because, at the very moment when "America was discovered," the long, agonizing hour of dealing with the little "angels" was also up.

It was an extremely difficult beginning, but later, as the children grew more used to us, and we to them, we were able to control and organize them in spite of the great numbers. Even my gentle companion, with her sweet disposition, came to be loved and respected by those children. That mission became a major project of multitudes, with everything in huge quantities, for, during the summer, we worked in a camp with thousands of children. The fire department lent us tents where we offered arts and crafts of all kinds for children of all ages. Both the children and we religious had a wonderful time. The camps were open an entire month; that experience taught me a great deal about discipline and organization (a tremendous asset when I would be called upon later to coordinate the myriad youth programs we would one day establish in the Playa de Ponce). I learned much about the young.

I remember particularly a group of young women with whom we used to take walks in the park, and visit museums and historical sites. We had the opportunity to talk for long hours, and I came to know of their concerns, dreams, frustrations, and interests. We formed a missionary cenacle through which they helped us teach catechism and visit the sick on Welfare Island. (This is a small island located between Brooklyn and Manhattan where the government housed the poorest people.)

As I said above, everything we did had a certain hugeness about it: the great spaghetti fair we organized is one example. Sister Louise cooked pot after pot of spaghetti; it was an immense quantity. A huge amount was sold, but the leftovers were also overwhelming. For the next few weeks we were eating spaghetti for breakfast, lunch, and supper. I could hardly stand to look at spaghetti anymore, and would have done anything for some rice.

Our lives and ministry progressed quite peacefully until one night when I felt a sharp pain. The sisters called the motherhouse suspecting it might be appendicitis. The general custodian directed that I go to Philadelphia so that the doctors who looked after the congregation might examine me. Dutifully, I set off for Philadelphia. I remember that, as I was about to board a subway car, I was shocked when the doors opened to find myself face to face with my brother, Luis; his amazement was greater still, since he didn't even know I was in New York. We sat together for a moment and, when I told him the reason I was going to Philadelphia, he could not believe it and said: "That's crazy; how can they send you on a trip by train if you have appendicitis? I'm going to call a doctor friend here in New York and I'll call your general custodian to authorize your receiving treatment here."

I responded: "Do what you think best, but I ought to continue my journey as I was told." And so I went on my way. In Philadelphia, the doctor chose to keep me under observation for a few days because he was not sure what I had. At that point Luis called the general custodian to tell her he had a doctor and had made all the necessary arrangements for my care. She answered him very sweetly, saying that he should not worry because I was the responsibility of the congregation, but he would not give in. They talked on the phone for quite a while until she finally told him that they would send me by train to Alabama where our community had a hospital. That was all he needed to hear; my brother almost hit the roof. But in the end he had to accept the decision of the congregation, and I set out for Alabama with the general custodian.

On the train we were both put in one narrow bed, but with the motion of the train and the pain I was experiencing, neither one of us got a wink of sleep. Upon arriving at the hospital, we found no one available to assist us since a special celebration was in progress that was to last three days. Meanwhile, my siblings were driving the sisters crazy, calling two or three times a day to find out what was going on with me. I tried to calm them by saying I was no longer in pain, but they were not satisfied.

Finally, the days of celebration were over and when the doctor examined me, he decided to operate. Immediately the congregation called my family. It was war time and it wasn't easy to book flights, but Saro succeeded in having Herman secure seats for them both in a plane filled with soldiers. Thanks to Herman, Saro was able to endure the flight with relative calm as she was terrified of planes. They arrived two days after the surgery and found me sitting up in bed. On seeing me, Saro exclaimed: "Heavens, what are you doing sitting up after an operation?" But times had changed, and no longer did post-operative patients have to remain prone in bed for long periods of time. I gave thanks to God because, as a result of my illness, I was able to see three of my siblings. I recuperated rapidly and was soon back at work.

I truly enjoyed my three years in Long Island City, but in November 1946 I was sent to another mission which filled me with great joy because I was to return to my native land, Puerto Rico, to work with my own people, as I had so much desired.

CABO ROJO (NOVEMBER 1946–1955)

His Excellency Aloysius J. Willinger, bishop of Ponce, had asked our congregation to come to work in Cabo Rojo because problems had arisen among the workers in the salt pans and they were on strike. Cabo Rojo was an essentially Catholic town and the Church was afraid that the Communists might take advantage of these conflicts to infiltrate the townspeople. We arrived in Cabo Rojo on a Sunday. There were three of us: Sister Eucarista, a young Puerto Rican; Sister Miriam, an elderly sister from the States, and I. I shall never forget that day. It was the first time that our congregation had come to Cabo Rojo, and the entire town turned out to give us a royal welcome that included a musical band. It was a happy day both for them and for us.

After the great welcome, they brought us to what would be our cenacle, a small house that seemed made for dolls. It had no porch so that, on stepping out the door, we found ourselves directly on the street. Because the bathroom and kitchen were located in the back yard, our dear neighbors always knew exactly who was doing each day's cooking, and when each of us went to the bathroom. Actually, this was no great problem for us, especially for Sister Eucarista and myself who were so pleased to be working for the first time in our own country.

We immediately began to work with the children and, through them, we came to know their parents and relatives.

Before we realized it, we were organizing baseball teams. The mothers offered to make uniforms; some of the boys on the team who were apprenticed to tailors sewed their own. (Cabo Rojo was a town with a great reputation for excellent tailors). The uniforms were made from sugar sacks; to distinguish one team from the other, we would trim them in different bright colors. The games were played on Sundays, but first we would go to Mass. Our friends who had trucks for transporting sugar cane, would lend us their trucks so that we could transport the children. They were open trucks, and the children and sisters would climb into them. We came and returned singing and enjoying the countryside. Each team had its own color and name, and some names they were! These included: Saint Michael's Team; Saint Joseph's Team; Saint Louis's Team, etc. On Sundays the people who came to watch them play would cry out: "Come on, you saints come down from Heaven; play ball!" I remember one of the players with great affection; we used to call him "Canena" because he was dark-skinned like the famous Puerto Rican player "Canena" Márquez. He was an enormous boy and his uniform was too tight. During one game, as he slid into a base, an unmistakable ripping noise resounded through the air, and we knew the poor boy's uniform had come apart on his ample rear end. He jumped up like lightning, uncovered for all to see; the game had to stop for quite a while, because no one, himself included, could control their hysterical laughter.

Besides the ball games, we used to take field trips so as to become acquainted with other towns and cities on the island, including Ponce, Aibonito, and San Juan. At the same time we had to fulfill our main objectives, which were: teaching religion and the Bible, giving talks on topics of interest, dialoguing with our students, and providing guidance. They responded to these activities with the same interest they manifested in playing ball and taking trips. I imagine their response was so good because we were helping them to channel their energies in activities that gave them great satisfaction.

We also spent time visiting the tiny mountain villages. There were places we could not reach by car and after a certain point we had to continue by ox-cart. Sometimes, when we returned in the evening, our habits were muddied almost to our waists. But the effort was worthwhile because after each mission, the pastor would accompany us and baptize many children, witness the marriage of many couples, and give Holy Communion to a large number. For all, it was an unforgettable joy and celebration.

The people of Cabo Rojo loved us very much and had a great deal of respect for us. I recall the unpleasant experience I once had when the police almost made us lose the friendship and good relations we enjoyed with the townspeople. The decade of the fifties had begun and the government was quite worried that the Puerto Rican Nationalist Party might stage a violent coup to proclaim independence from the United States. I was at that time the custodian of our cenacle. One day the police came and asked us for our red bus because, according to them, they had an emergency. Without asking them what the emergency was, we innocently lent it to them. On the following day, my indignation knew no bounds when I learned that they had used the bus to arrest and carry off to Mayagüez those of our people who were members of the Nationalist party, people whom we knew to be harmless. The only thing I could do to undo the damage and recover the people's trust was to visit each family, express my apologies, and take them some food.

Thank God that the incident, the only one of its kind, did not destroy our standing in the town of Cabo Rojo, and so the years passed very fruitfully until the moment came to say good-bye. Today, I realize that our efforts were not wasted, because the majority of our young people are now teachers, lawyers, and doctors. Many years after leaving Cabo Rojo, while I was walking along a New York street, a young man pulled up in his car along the curb and said to me: "Sister, do you remember me? I'm Canena, one of the players in your 'celestial' teams in Cabo Rojo. I'm a doctor now. I'm married and have children. I would love to have you come by my office."

I left Cabo Rojo with deep sorrow. I had enjoyed great satisfaction each day in our dealings with people who were simple, humble, and so easy to love.

RIO PIEDRAS (AUGUST 1955)

I arrived in Río Piedras unaware of the storm that awaited me. I had been named custodian of the Trinitarian sisters at the cenacle in Hato Rey; furthermore, I had been appointed religion teacher in the School of Our Lady of Mercy. I found the cenacle building in terrible shape. As I went over the papers and accounts of the congregation, I found a bank book that indicated a healthy balance in the savings account. After consulting with the community, all the sisters agreed that we should use the money for the repairs needed in our cenacle. Within a few days, that unkempt place in which we lived had new doors and shelving, as well as new mattresses on the beds and good food in the pantry.

I found the work there difficult and tedious. In the morning I had a tight schedule of religion classes. At noon I had to wash habits, and so I had no time to visit people and chat with them. One day, while at the washing machine, I suffered a deep cut in one arm, but paid little attention to it. As time passed, the daily contact with dirty water infected the wound and I began to feel sick. One afternoon Luisita Torruella, a close friend, came to visit me and, upon seeing the wound, dragged me to the hospital on the spot. Thanks to my friend and to the penicillin I was given, the septicemia that had begun to invade my body yielded to treatment and I was soon well again.

As time passed, however, I became more and more isolated in silence and in the solitude of the house. Sadness and near-despair seem to take hold of my spirit. One day Sister Mary Paula Collazo, a friend from Caguas who loved me very much, came to visit me. My eyes could not hide the spiritual turmoil I was experiencing and she, perceiving it, tried to console me. But I was in such a state of depression that I needed something more than words, as well intentioned as hers were. Without my knowing it, she alerted our general custodian.

The day after my friend's visit, I received a call from the general custodian in Philadelphia. Our exchange could hardly be called a conversation; it was just a few words, and phrases which weren't even sentences—but this was enough to pull me out of that destructive, paralyzing inertia. The only thing she heard from me were the words: "I can't go on." And I remember her saying: "Take the next plane to Philadelphia and I will be waiting for you at the airport."

On the plane, my thoughts had lost all perspective, seemed to drown out all hope...I even lost the awareness of God. Upon arriving at the motherhouse, I went directly to the chapel reserved for the sick because that was how I felt: sick within. As I knelt before the altar I noticed that the Blessed Sacrament was exposed there in the monstrance as was done on solemn occasions. I was amazed when I realized that the monstrance before me was the very one that was made, in part, with my mother's jewels and the small jewels I had received at my First Communion and for my fifteenth birthday celebration. (In Puerto Rico a girl's fifteenth birthday is a special occasion much like the "sweet sixteen" in the States.) I had donated those jewels to the congregation the day I had entered the cenacle with such high hopes.

At that moment in the chapel, my life seemed to pass before my eyes. I could see that my life, from childhood, had been directed by my father's and my mother's good works, by my visits to the poor friends of Pellín, by the shoe-shine boys, by Cariño, by that happy Canena in his split uniform...by Father Thomas Judge; directed toward what I was now, a Missionary Servant of the poor. I tried to recollect myself, and took out from my missal the letter that Father Judge had sent me when, during my adolescence, I was convalescing in Adjuntas:

"My dear child...The Divine Architect has a plan for your life, and each day, His mysterious Providence continues to weave this tapestry of incomparable beauty for His Honor and Glory, for your happiness and for the good of your neighbor.... Can anything or anyone interfere or spoil the design? There is danger of interference, of damage, and this danger comes, in great part, from ourselves. We become impatient with the way in which God does things. Our fanciful desires and restless moods cause us to resist the necessary restrictions of the Divine Sculptor, and perversely, and even insanely at times, we want another design, a design more to our liking. What a shame it would be if our perversity were to prevail! See, therefore, the value of being patient. What a beautiful doctrine the Lord gave us, what secret joy is found in His words: "Sufficient for the day is the evil thereof" (Mt 6:34). The thread of the marvelous design in your life is beginning to appear. It is rapturously beautiful. It makes one stand in awe. I ask myself if even you yourself can perceive it. Be aware that there is a beautiful providence that is working in your life. You can begin to follow the imprint in the hand of the Divine Artist....

The Holy Spirit has all that you lack, be that spiritual or corporal. You need the Holy Spirit because you have needs that are spiritual and corporal. You have great spiritual aspirations. You have a desire for perfection. You wish to do a great deal for Jesus. You look for good health.... The Holy Spirit is as marvelous with the body as with the soul. It is He who finishes and perfects. There is no color, nor fragrance in a beautiful flower that was not put there by the Holy Spirit. He brings about the harvest. He forms and molds and beautifies and gives health to the body. These days are valuable for you...because the Holy Spirit is so disposed to hear the innocent and the pure of heart and those who love Him."

(Letter from Father Judge to Isolina, July 14, 1933)

Then I saw it clearly. *I was interfering in the work God was doing in my life; I had lost patience with God.* A moment of suspenseful silence followed as the weight that seemed to be dragging my soul in a downward spiral began to lift. In rapid succession the pain I had been feeling gave way to tears flowing from eyes now tired from looking within at my own misery. Life was going on as usual outside that chapel, but inside it, time had ceased to exist in some mysterious fashion. As I left the chapel I could not decide if hours or minutes had passed or if I had died and been reborn. (God seems to have a special way of provoking supernatural incidents without making anyone, but the person concerned, aware of what He is doing. For this, if for no other reason, I cannot but believe in Him). The Sister Thomas Marie (Isolina) who walked out the doors of the chapel, was quite another; in no sense was she the same one who had entered a few minutes earlier...or was it hours before, or a century? On the other hand, she was the same physically and unchanged in other ways: out-going, joyful...; but, spiritually a great change had occurred within, which made my self-donation to the Lord more genuine, more conscious. It might be compared with what happens when a young couple renew their loving commitment after a crisis has almost separated them forever.

I was ordered to rest. That period of rest lasted about six months. It was 1955, the Marian Year, and I was sent with two sisters to visit Lourdes, in France. Upon my return to Philadelphia, I was sent to study English literature and other courses at Holy Family University which was near the motherhouse. (As it happens, I was to be honored in 1991 with a doctorate, *honoris causa* by that very university.) I studied there until the summer of 1956, when Monsignor Ivan Illich, at the time vice-rector of the Catholic University in Ponce, invited me to participate in a cultural seminar at which I was to speak about the character and customs of Puerto Ricans to a group of American priests and religious, who would then return to the States to work among Puerto Ricans. The experience was quite surprising to me. I remember that Father Joseph Fitzpatrick, a Jesuit priest and sociologist from Fordham University, was present and, although he knew me already as a woman of action, he had serious doubts as to my ability to speak effectively. When he noticed that I was indeed the speaker, he leapt from his seat with the speed of lightning and, dashing over to a friend of his, a very scholarly sister who was also present at the conference, asked her to sit in the front row and, as soon as I began to stammer, to go to the podium and take over from me. Meanwhile, he did not feel he could bear to witness the expected "catastrophe"; so he left the hall, took out his rosary and began to pray,...(like the Columbus of my story). I don't know if it was his prayers or that my talents as a public speaker had, until then, gone unrecognized, or perhaps both, but the talk was a great success and everyone seemed very pleased with my presentation.

On my return to Philadelphia, I decided to visit my friend, Sister Mary Tonra, at the Dr. White Settlement Center in Brooklyn. There I remained without ever having planned it that way.

Our founder, Father Thomas Judge, had opened the Dr. White Settlement Association in 1915, when the great wave of Italian immigration arrived in the United States. Dr. White was a tireless social worker and a great priest. The house that was to serve as our cenacle was given to the congregation on a temporary basis, but with time, it became permanent.

Sister Tonra and Sister Ann, another friend of mine, were studying at Saint Joseph's College for Women in Brooklyn. Since the congregation had not yet decided what to do with me after my crisis, my friends suggested that I go to study with them. I liked the idea and asked for the necessary permission, which was granted.

BROOKLYN (1956–1968)

I began my studies for a bachelor's degree in September, 1956 and finished them in December, 1958. During that time I was offered a position as a volunteer at the Dr. White

Center, and I accepted. During the time that was left at my disposal after my classes, I worked among the Hispanic people. In January of 1959 I was called to Philadelphia to give a course in conversational Spanish to twenty-five novices. I had not studied to be a teacher, but since the request had come from the motherhouse, I could not refuse. I asked for guidance from a teacher I had had and set off for Philadelphia as prepared as I could be. Classes were held every day, since I had to cover an entire year in one semester. Surprisingly, the goal was achieved, and the American novices left speaking Spanish, although I had damaged their English accent after they were forced to listen to my brand of accented English.

I developed my own teaching style, which the novices seemed to like very much. I taught them by making use of all the songs and games of our folklore: for example, *Arroz con leche, La cojita que mi nu fli* and *A mamá que le mande una cebollita.* We all had a wonderful time. I also spoke so much to them about Puerto Rico, its beauty, and our people, that at the end of their novitiate, they asked the general custodian to send them to Puerto Rico on mission. After my work with the novices, I returned to the Catholic University of Puerto Rico to repeat the talk I had previously given there. This time, the general custodian was present during my talk and suggested that I study for a master's degree. I began my studies at Fordham with Father Fitzpatrick. Instead of studying social work as my companions were doing, I studied sociology. At about that time (1959) I was named director of the Dr. White Settlement Center, since the former director had left to pursue further studies.

Surrounding the Center was a housing complex consisting of ten buildings in each of which 144 families lived; the complex was called The Farragut Project. At first, as I have indicated, most of the residents had been Italian, but by the

76

time I entered the picture, the population was more varied, composed—in varying proportions—of Blacks and Puerto Ricans with a few Italians and Jews.

At the same time that I began my work among the so-called minorities, visiting them and organizing them, I was continuing my graduate studies and entering the intellectual world of that period. I met Dorothy Dohen and Father Robert Fox, worked with them and with Ivan Illich, John Martin, Father Joseph Fitzpatrick, and Gordon J. Klopf. I also enrolled in the Bank Street College of Education. It was interesting to be learning the theory and, at the same time, working with the reality; the theories that worked remained, those that did not were cast aside.

When I was named director of the program, I had to appear before the Board of Directors of the Dr. White Center to advise them of my appointment, and to inform them of the economic data that the outgoing director had asked me to give them. The directors were not from that part of Brooklyn where we worked, but from an exclusive sector of the city. Many were Irish, some were Italian, and others were German, but almost all were intellectuals or wives of business leaders.

Although I was a religious sister, the first thing they noted, not favorably, was that I was Puerto Rican. The second thing that left a negative impression was my hopeless English pronunciation. As I read to them from the financial report in which were listed amounts in the thousands of dollars, I gave the sound of "s" to every "th." The women listening almost passed out. The more I continued to pronounce "sousands," the more nervous and upset they became. At first their nervousness made me nervous, but I was determined to proceed courageously because my goal was to bring about change in the way the Board worked. They used to hold their meetings in other locations and never even looked in to see the reality of what went on at the Center. I wanted to teach them that Catholic Christians, such as they were, had the obligation of sharing with Catholic Christians like the Blacks and the Puerto Ricans and the Italians who were served at the Center.

In the end, I achieved this goal. It was not easy but, little by little, I got them to move their meetings to the Center; to visit the families we served; and finally even to volunteer to serve as tutors to the children and teenagers. It was a great experience to see these two social classes become integrated. I remember how the wife of a judge from the Family Court of the City was able to convince her husband (a very refined Irishman) to take a boy from the Center fishing every week.

In this way I became interested and involved in the problems of minorities and in the struggle for civil rights, and before I knew it, the mayor of New York City, John Lindsay, named me to the Committee of the War on Poverty. This was a great personal achievement for me, since no one, not even the mayor, knew me by my real name, or was aware of my family's political importance in Puerto Rico. To them I was simply Sister Thomas Marie. During this time I learned how to operate in political situations.

The decade of the seventies saw the founding of the Puerto Rican Forum from which ASPIRA was born. This gave me the opportunity to work with successful Puerto Ricans such as Dr. Francisco Trilla, Antonia Pantoja, Blanca Cedeño, Luis Alvarez, and many others. It was a period of very intense experiences. On the one hand, while these persons and I struggled for the rights of Puerto Ricans, we did not hesitate to identify with other similar struggles. During and after the sixties, Blacks, Hispanics, and all minorities were reclaiming their civil rights. I lived through racial conflicts like those on the East Side. I also involved myself in the politics of the day, even though I was not a politician. I learned what it meant to be a Democrat or a Republican, although I myself did not identify with either. Nelson Rockefeller offered his help, but in political terms we did not work in the same style. I learned to prepare effective and successful proposals. In a word, the work and the learning went on constantly.

From a religious standpoint, the Catholic Church was experiencing very important changes, some very positive and others somewhat negative; I refer to the revolution wrought by the Second Vatican Council which brought with it an openness in the Church for greater participation of the laity in the liturgy and the evangelization of peoples. It also led many Sisters to return to our baptismal names. After answering to the name Sister Thomas Marie for so many years, it was at first a little difficult to respond to the name Sister María Isolina. However, it was only a matter of becoming accustomed to it once again. Many cloistered congregations opened their doors and came out into the world to evangelize it; others who had been dedicated to working primarily with upper social classes decided to walk with the poor, bringing to them the Good News of the Gospel. One of the changes that most touched us was the manner in which we were assigned our missions. Previously, we were given assignments that had been thought about, prayed over, meditated, and discerned; since Vatican II, the general custodian (in the case of our congregation), dialogues and speaks with the sister concerned, taking into consideration her inclinations, opinions, and feelings. After the dialogue, and both personal and communal prayer and discernment, the decision is made.

It was an era of pressures of all kinds. Working with the young at that time was not easy. There was a great deal of delinquency, and to help delinquent youths effectively and gain their confidence, one almost had to become, so to speak, their accomplice. One night we religious were about to retire when we heard loud screams. Looking out the window, we saw a teenager running in apparent fright and taking shelter at our doorstep. He began to ring the bell desperately while calling out: "Sisters, open up or they'll kill me!" Without a second thought, we ran to the door and opened it. The boy came in, and no sooner had we closed the door behind him than a large gang of young men appeared looking to kill him. Thankfully, they were not aware that we had taken him in, but they continued to prowl around the area waiting for him to come out of hiding. The night continued on its course, but those delinquents refused to leave the area. We could not decide what to do: if we were to call the police the gang would discover that we were harboring an enemy of theirs; on the other hand, the teenager we were protecting could not remain in the cenacle because he was a man. Suddenly I got an idea, and half an hour later I drove out with the young man seated in the passenger seat of our car next to me. As we drove past the gang they were totally unaware that their enemy was with me. They saw only me and another "nun" in the car because I had dressed him up in one of our habits. We had saved his life and still kept the trust of everyone involved.

So many were the intense experiences I lived through during those memorable years that I think I could write a book just on my time in Brooklyn. I never tire of thanking God for allowing me to be a part of a process of learning and growth that was at once so complicated and so delicate. All the years of working in different states around the country gave me the opportunity to come to know all types of human beings, their strengths and weaknesses, their aspirations and preoccupations. Some people were so radically different from each other that it was difficult to figure out how they could coexist in the same geographical area. Yet, based on many years of working with people, I am convinced that, in spite of all the differences, human beings have at least one essential characteristic in common: the desire, conscious or unconscious, to attain the fullness of life. With that conviction clearly formed, I left Brooklyn and the United States and arrived at the Playa de Ponce.

The Playa

The glory of God is man and woman fully alive. *(A free translation of words by St. Ireneus)*

God has created me for his glory and, consequently, the only way I can give him glory is to make certain that this creation which is myself, be, within inevitable limits, as good as it can be, that is, that I live a full life, that I be totally and generously myself...Our goal must be to raise the level of our existence to panoramas higher than nature and grace; to live a full life so as to give God complete glory."

Anthony de Mello, S.J.

After twenty-two years of missionary work in the continental United States, on a memorable day, July 22, 1968, I was notified that I would be sent to my native land, Puerto Rico, to work among my own people. My joy was even greater when I learned that it would be to my native town that I was to go to serve as a missionary. "You are assigned to the Playa de Ponce—the Ponce waterfront area—where you will work with our sisters who have been there since 1950." I thanked God for such an undeserved gift. I was also named custodian of the community. At that juncture of my life I had become quite a different person. During the previous twenty-two years I had acquired skills in community organizing, established connections with governmental agencies and political groups, and established some expertise in the administration and maintenance of non-profit organizations. All of this, of course, was in the

Sister Isolina with children from La Playa de Ponce.

A model to the children: Chichi Rodriguez, our famous golf player, also came from a public housing project. Here he shares with the children of Centros Sor Isolina with encouragement and love.

Sister Isolina receiving the Albert Schweitzer Award from Johns Hopkins University in 1989.

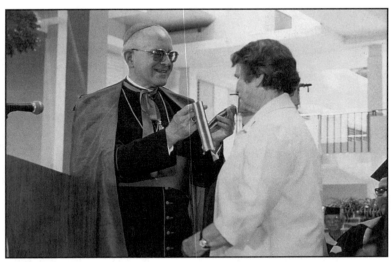

Sister Isolina receiving an award from the Bishop of Ponce given to her by the Catholic University of Puerto Rico.

84

Sister Isolina and children of La Playa de Ponce.

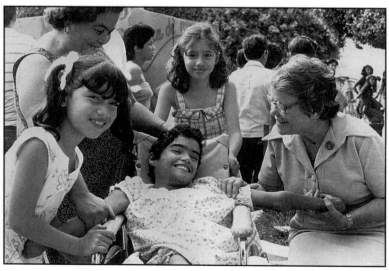

Sister Isolina working with the handicapped children.

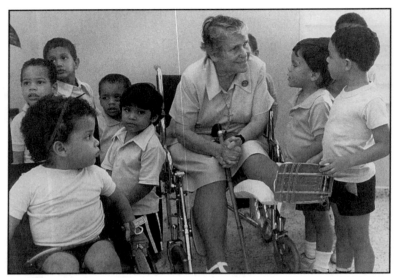

Sister Isolina sharing with some of the handicapped children from the Center.

Centro Sor Isolina Ferré as it is today.

interest of the poor so that they might become aware of their personal dignity that should be respected, and that they should respect themselves. The experiences I had had in the United States strengthened in me the compassion I had always felt for the helplessness of the poor in general.

Before anything else, however, I was ordered to take a rest, for I had been working almost without pause since I had been assigned to Brooklyn in 1956. It seems, nevertheless, that God sometimes enjoys contradicting orders to rest. I had scarcely arrived at the Playa when I experienced an urgency to go out immediately and become better acquainted with it. As a child I had visited the Playa, but only in passing and for pleasure. I began now to walk its paths, paths that, without my knowing it at that moment, would become my special place, my Playa. That day as I walked through its streets and alleys, my heart seemed to contract as I discovered the misery and abandonment to which my people had been subjected. It was as if I saw them drowning, hopelessly, into a thick and malodorous quicksand. In speaking with the residents of the Playa, I came to realize that, in general, they did not have the slightest idea that there might be better alternatives for their lives. They were not even aware of the help that the government could offer them. The condition of their health was precarious and the Playa had the highest rate of juvenile delinquency (17.8 percent) among all the neighborhoods of Ponce. As I passed through their unpaved alleys, I noticed that many of the zinc ceilings on their wooden shacks were covered with stones. In questioning the residents, I discovered that the reason was that the boys, upon returning home, were so filled with pent-up anger that they would throw stones to vent their frustration, finding themselves unable to communicate satisfactorily with their parents. I recall one particular sector known by the name of "Las Cucarachas"("the Cockroaches") and asked the reason for that name. A gentleman, who happened to be a veteran of the Second World War, explained that one of the families that lived there was so large (and every now and then grew larger) that they were called "the cockroaches"; with time the entire area acquired the same nickname.

During my tour I passed by the Dispensario San Antonio, founded by my father, Antonio Ferré, in 1950. It was a small clinic presided over by the Missionary Servants of the Most Blessed Trinity, and the only place the residents of the Playa could count on to monitor the health of their children. At the time of my return, its services were no longer adequate to the increased needs of the area. In the rest of the Playa, there was not a single doctor, nurse, or dentist on full-time duty and accessible to them, nor were there any social agencies or other health centers. As a result, health conditions were deplorable, and infant mortality very high. This was the Playa I found after twenty-five years away from Puerto Rico. The situation was sufficiently critical to make anyone feel discouraged and helpless. In essence, the Playa was a community in which people did not live life to the full.

By nightfall, I decided to end my walk and return to the cenacle; I was feeling physically, mentally and emotionally exhausted. On the way home I began to reflect upon how I might face and deal with this situation. It seemed to me that an urgent response was required to remedy the poverty and the loss of life and opportunities evident all around me. My heart dictated such a course of action. It was imperative that I apply the knowledge and skills I had acquired during my missionary life to helping the people of the Playa. Fortunately, there were other people interested in improving that sad situation, but they did not know how to go about it. Now it was that the vision, previously alluded to, acquired new urgency. I had been trying to develop it all my life by means of the experiences God had permitted me to live; it was now, at that crucial moment, that it became a palpable reality. I had one thing going for me: I was no longer alone, since there were many other committed people willing to struggle with me to make the Playa a better place. We all desired one thing: that every inhabitant of the Playa should become a person fully alive within a vibrant community.

That night, upon retiring, I felt my heart beat more rapidly as my thoughts raced from one idea, one plan, to the other. Physically, I felt exhausted and had to recover my strength. But as I closed my eyes, all the scenes I had witnessed during the day—the despairing faces of the men and women of the Playa, the sick children and those who played in the streets because there were no schools for them to attend—emerged on the screen of my memory. I remembered the almost prophetic words of Father Thomas Augustine Judge spoken while I was convalescing in Adjuntas during the illness I had contracted in adolescence: "My child, get well...there are many children who need you." Who could have imagined that those simple but demanding words would be fulfilled like a prophecy prompted and inspired by God himself? That night I said to God my Father: "I cannot go off for a rest after what I have seen today. I want to help these people. This is a need I feel; it's even keeping me awake. I want to be one of them, one of these good people who do not recognize their own capabilities and potential to attain the fullness of their lives. I want to be Your instrument to help them find themselves and to discover their value as human beings. I want these people, so truly Yours, to be mine also. I want that this, Your Playa, be my Playa also. Give me Your strength and Your repose...." After this face-to-face encounter with God, I was able to close my eyes serenely and not open them again until the following morning when I awakened relaxed, happy, and so charged up with energy that I could scarcely contain myself. After two weeks of rest, which were enough time to prepare me physically and mentally to undertake my new charge, I began to walk the new path that I still walk today.

I called a meeting of community leaders to discuss alternative strategies to address the difficult and pressing problems of our Playa. The night of the meeting, however, I was ill and unable to attend. Later, my sister companions told me it had not been a fruitful meeting because the community leaders present were political activists, each pushing his own agenda and refusing to compromise for the good of the Playa. I then decided to call another meeting of leaders, but this time I consulted with the residents of the area who really knew the strengths and needs of the Playa and, above all, who loved it. I remember with great affection the minister of the Methodist Church, Rev. Julita Torres Fernández; the elderly veteran from the Cucarachas district who had explained its name; Alfonso Sánchez, a *playero*, (the name by which those who lived in the Playa were called), who was secretary of Ferré Industries and who would provide secretarial assistance to us; the Masons of the Faro de la Marina Lodge, and many more. The members of the Puerto Viejo Social Club were also a great help, since they were very familiar with the needs of the *playeros*. We dialogued and dialogued, arriving finally at certain important conclusions: the people of the Playa needed to learn about the various government agencies which could help them solve their diverse problems. We also realized that the idleness that had taken possession of the *playeros* was the result of the fact that, after the recent closing of the docks, the men bereft of other marketable skills had been left in a state of inertia that was dangerous, not just to themselves, but to their families and, indeed, to the entire community. We also saw that the playera women felt helpless, unfulfilled, and inwardly yearning to do something for themselves and their families.

I wanted to move the meeting along in such a way that solutions might come from the residents, and so it happened. The Rev. Julita Torres said: "Let's establish a center where guidance and other services might be offered." We all liked the idea. "It will be called Center of Orientation and Services, and we'll begin in two weeks," she concluded. Within two weeks, just as Doña Julita had "ordered," we inaugurated our center. Much of our guidance was done out of doors. We would go, for example, to one sector, and the people would bring out chairs from their small houses and form a small open-air auditorium. The *playeros* would discuss their needs with us, and we would direct them to the specific governmental agency they could call upon. We offered these services on the first floor of our cenacle located on Padre Noel Avenue. I recall that my good friend, Sister Mary Paula Collazo, director of Ponce's Head Start Program, sent us two of her teachers. They came to us after completing their own day's work. The husband of one of them, Mr. Lans, worked in a clothing factory and was able to obtain for us some industrial-type sewing machines. With them we began our first workshop for professional seamstresses, where both women and girls found work. In like manner, we initiated cooking classes with a stove I had acquired from a kind benefactor. At this point an obvious need brought us to another service, when we noticed that the women who were taking the classes did not know how to read or write and, as a result, could not write down the recipes the teachers were giving them. It was then that I remembered my classmates from Sacred Heart Academy in Ponce who were now married and living comfortably at home. I gathered a few of them and asked them the following question: "What are you doing sitting at home when there are so many people in the Playa with so many needs?" Several joined me as we began a literacy program directed by Sister Rosita María Bauzá.

I remember Isabel, a young woman who could neither read nor write and was among the first to sign up for the course. She used to feel ashamed when she had to go to the bank and had to sign documents with an X because it was the only thing she knew how to write. Our course lasted three months, and that's how long it took her to learn how to write her full name. After three months we held our first graduation for the first literacy group. I included Isabel's name in this first group and was asked why I was giving a diploma to someone who had merely learned to write her name. I can still remember my answer: "Because she no longer has to experience the humiliation of having to write a cold and impersonal X instead of her name." When we gave her the diploma, Isabel received it with great pride and joy. I shall never forget the look of pleasure on her face when, a few days later, she came to the Center to tell us that she finally had been able to sign her name during the transactions at the bank.

The men of the Playa also troubled us very much. They had been accustomed to working on the docks, and these were the only jobs for which they had any skills. When the docks closed, they were left up in the air, not knowing what to do or where to go to become, once again, gainfully employed. Their pride and their dignity were sapped; they lost their self-respect. In their idleness and depression, many turned to vices such as drinking or gambling while others abused their families. One day I voiced my fears about them to Teodoro Moscoso who originated the slogan "Operation Bootstrap," used popularly by Governor Luis Muñoz Marín, and who had been the director of that island-wide industrialization project for many years. Mr. Moscoso's reaction was: "Why don't you train them in welding? There is a great demand for solderers and welders these days." I responded: "How can we do this if we know nothing about welding and do not even have the means to set up the necessary equipment?" He smiled and said to me: "I'll provide the trainers and the equipment, and you make sure the men attend the classes."

Within a short time we set up the needed space, donated by the Puerto Rico Iron Works, and announced the inauguration of the Antonio Ferré School of the Arts and Industrial Skills. We so named it because my father used to tell us that a man should not just learn a skill that would provide him with economic sustenance, but had an obligation to develop his creativity by means of the arts. Now the playeros would become skilled in welding and in carpentry which we introduced later, while the women learned to use the sewing machine for industrial purposes.

We took advantage of the first anniversary of the Center for Orientation and Services to inaugurate the vocational school. That day one of the invited guests was my brother Luis who was then governor of Puerto Rico. He brought along with him almost all the members of his cabinet. I think it was the first time that a governor of Puerto Rico had come to the Playa with all the secretaries of the various governmental departments. Also present was the bishop of Ponce, the Most Rev. Fremiot Torres Oliver. The latter was so moved by the work being done at the Center with such scarce resources, that he removed his episcopal ring and gave it to me to sell for the benefit of the Center. We were all touched by such a noble gesture. Some remembered that in the early nineteenth century, the first native bishop of Puerto Rico, Don Juan Alejo de Arizmendi had also given his episcopal ring to Don Ramón Power, who was sailing to Spain as Puerto Rico's first representative at the

Spanish Cortes (Parliament). Now, several persons who were present, upon seeing the bishop's generous gesture, approached me and gave me double the monetary worth of the ring with the proviso that I keep it so as to one day exhibit it in the Museum of Art in commemoration of his selfless gesture.

That day, in the midst of so much emotion, a very funny thing happened when the lady in charge of presenting a bouquet of flowers to my brother Luis became flustered and, instead of correctly saying Luis' name, she called him by the name of the previous governor, his long-time rival, Don Luis Muñoz Marín. All present, starting with my brother, let out a great laugh, except for the poor lady, who was utterly mortified by her faux pas. When my brother spoke, he said: "This has happened to me several times; and I always take the opportunity to stress that Don Luis Muñoz Marín ought to be remembered by all Puerto Ricans because of his great achievements as governor." These words so touched those present that they gave him a great ovation. Luis has always supported me in all my projects as did my other brothers, now deceased. His wife, Lorencita, who is also reposing with the Lord, always followed with interest the evolution of my vision and, even from her sick bed, never failed to encourage us in our work.

In the Playa, the large school drop-out rate, along with juvenile delinquency, threatened to destroy our children and teenagers. Fortunately, I was visited by my friends from my Brooklyn days: John Martin, Gordon Klopf, and Joseph Fitzpatrick. I shared with them my concerns about our youth and, as I recall, one of them said: "There's a new concept being discussed in the United States for working with young delinquents called, in English, "advocacy."

"What does that mean?" I inquired curiously.

Father Fitzpatrick explained it to me: "Advocacy means

simply selecting good young people and adults living in the same community as the delinquents who can then serve as mediators between them and the courts; thus, a workable accord can be reached so that the delinquents do not go to jail but are empowered to change, mend their ways, and be reintegrated into their communities."

I was fascinated by this new concept. We decided to meet and discuss it with the Honorable Eugenio Velásquez Martín of the juvenile court and with other authorities such as the police and the Department of Education. As we described the new idea, all were impressed and agreed to support it; there remained only to find an expression in Spanish that would convey all its implications. After searching diligently in our mental files, the most appropriate word we could conjure up in Spanish was *intercesor*. Thanks to all concerned, we began this advocacy project, which today is one of the most solid pillars of our centers. It is as effective today as when it began. Thousands of young people have benefited from this program and have been rescued from the premature death that would have resulted from their involvement with drugs and other criminal behavior.

Among so many, I especially remember Juan, one of the first to avail himself of the program. He was a young man, the father of a family, who had been jailed for selling drugs. After completing the term imposed by law and being freed, he returned to his house in the Playa, but was not accepted by his family. He then came to us and we received him. (Perhaps the memory of Juan has not been erased from my mind because I relate it to a memory from my childhood, when the young boy named Guadalupe appeared one afternoon at my parent's door weeping because his family did not want him in their home.) Juan worked on the docks, and would visit us, willing to accept our assistance, he soon offered to collaborate with us. He understood all too well the world of the delinquents, and knew how to confront them so as to make them react, look at things from a different angle, and change their ways. He was very tough and firm in the sessions in which he confronted the young people, but his intervention was invaluable. Juan came to share and make his own our commitment to work for a better Playa. Today there are many men and women who are grateful to Juan for having made them angry at him by confronting them at a crucial moment in their lives, because thanks to his intervention they are now upstanding members of their communities.

As a complement to this project, we developed others that became like magnets to attract the playeros to the center. We formed a steel band which we used as "bait" to attract the people; we organized a soccer team and offered a course in photography. We also opened, almost as a preventive measure, a recreation center which we called El Rincón Playero (The Playero Corner) "where good friends can meet." There young people could watch television, play table games and billiards, and speak with skilled personnel who could offer them professional guidance and advice. In this manner, when the young people got out of school, they had a safe place to go to enjoy themselves and to receive guidance if they had problems.

I never tired of looking for help and opportunities for my playeros. I recall one occasion when a distinguished gentleman, who had a camera and a photography business, was visiting us, and I made my usual pitch: "Why don't you donate some of your little Polaroid cameras to us so that the boys of the Playa might learn to take pictures?" He smiled and said indulgently: "With pleasure. Although I regret not being able to give you the competition's product, I will give you what I sell. I will send you forty Kodak cameras." "My God," as the kids would say, "What a haul!" But what counted was that the man understood our need and donated the cameras we needed.

But now, what were we going to do with so many cameras? At times, one does not stop to think of the consequences resulting from the gifts we receive; where were we going to procure film? Still, Providence always comes to the aid of the simple of heart. A friend of ours had a friend who was knowledgeable about photography, and he took charge of setting us up. He was able to attract the best teachers we could have ever hoped for: Ed Miller and Robert Medina, both of San Juan. Every Saturday they would travel to Ponce to teach photography to our young people. They also helped us acquire the materials and photographic equipment that we needed. The help they gave our young people can never be repaid; we will never forget how they identified with our cause and sponsored us so wholeheartedly. They were two great advocates. Their ideas and instruction live on to this day in our young photographers. When Robert and Ed arrived, we set up an improvised dark room next to the Rincón Playero, in an old lavatory. The space now served two purposes: while it could still be used as a bathroom, it was also used for developing film.

In 1971 we opened the Tabaiba Extension of our center, and celebrated the religious profession of Sister Rosita María Bauzá. That same year the Villa del Carmen housing development began to be built on lands belonging to Mr. José Saurí, (or Siso, as we affectionately called him). He and I knew each other since his sister and I had been classmates in Sacred Heart Academy in Ponce. I went to visit him and said: "How would you like to donate a piece of land to us at Villa del Carmen, and build us a hall of about forty by eighty feet?" Actually, I had no idea what size the measurements I gave might have been, but it was what occurred to me at the moment and I asked for it. I thought he was taken aback for a moment by my request but, fixing his eyes on me, he answered: "Of course, Isolina." The very next day he stopped work on part of the Villa del Carmen development and sent me some workmen to start building the hall I had requested. Some time later, when I saw the enormous building that Siso had built us, I could understand his reaction when I gave him those measurements; and mind you, he had made it a bit smaller!

That same year we had another memorable experience. I had never been able to forget the Cucarachas district of the Playa. In that area, to get from one house to another, it was necessary to cross small and unsafe bridges built by the residents themselves. Their huts were built on a muddy and contaminated mangrove swamp. One day I decided to walk to the Ferré Industries where a very kind and generous American named Robert O'Brien worked, and I expressed to him my concerns about the deplorable conditions of certain sectors of the Playa. He told me not to worry because he would contact his good friend Dr. Karanousky, who was at the time one of the directors in the U.S. Public Health Service in Washington. Robert O'Brien kept his word. After a few weeks, we received a visit from Dr. Karanousky, accompanied by some of his staff, who wanted to see with their own eyes the situation of the playeros. We took him to the Cucarachas district and, as he was walking across one of those small improvised bridges, the poor man stepped on a badly placed piece of wood and slipped. Before we could rescue him from falling into those foul-smelling waters, he was standing ankle-deep in them, while we remained paralyzed with shock and embarrassment. (There were some who later said that I had deliberately pushed the slat so that he might receive a more "concrete" impression of the situation, but God knows that this was not the case.)

That same afternoon Dr. Karanousky requested a meeting with the community, and we immediately organized a gathering for that evening. More than a hundred people from the community showed up. Among them was a current professor at the Pontifical Catholic University of Puerto Rico, Carlos Méndez Santos who, as a playero, is the pride of our youth. He describes himself as "a native of the Palmita and Puerto Viejo, poor neighborhoods of the Playa." Yet he was determined to attain a difficult and challenging goal, and is today a distinguished professor. It was Carlos Méndez who translated the proceedings of the meeting into Spanish for the community leaders present, since Dr. Karanousky's presentation was in English. After a dialogue between the community and the doctor and his people, the latter offered us a health service budget of a million dollars! We all laughed in utter disbelief, for such a sum seemed to us pure fantasy. But a few weeks after his departure from Puerto Rico, Dr. Karanousky sent us a large album of photographs taken during his visit to the Playa and directed us straight to where the money he promised us might be procured. He assigned us technicians who specialized in grant proposals, they trained our personnel in drawing up effective proposals. The proposals were accepted and we were given nothing less than the million dollars Dr. Karanousky had offered us. With the money in hand, we spoke with the Commonwealth of Puerto Rico government which, at the time, was building what is today the famous Diagnostic and Treatment Center of the Playa de Ponce and we procured their help. A board of directors was formed, composed of members of the community; democratic elections for positions on the board were held in each sector of the Playa. Those elections proved to be a unique experience for me, especially when, after having trained the members, they later said to me at a meeting: "You don't have to talk so much anymore; you're only the president!" The leaders of our community were beginning to give evidence of their capacity to direct their own destiny.

Education was another one of my concerns; to see so many children not attending school, or dropping out, or being thrown out, was distressing. And there were too many such cases. I would ask myself: "How can I convince these children that learning can be a joy?" It then occurred to me to invite people who knew more than I about these matters, scholars in the field of education. We invited experts from the Department of Public Instruction of Puerto Rico, the Board of Education of New York, and of course, Father Fitzpatrick. We dialogued at length, discussing every possible solution to the problem of our school dropouts. We spoke about alternative education, methods, books, theories, and ideas. At the conclusion of our exchange, they left, and we remained in a hyperactive state, anxious to put into practice the many ideas we had come up with. One of the Puerto Rican educators who had participated in the discussion was Doña Mariana Suárez de Longo who said to me: "I know a teacher who can help you with this undertaking because he has just the right qualities for this specific task. His name is Néstor Murray-Irrizary." Not resting for a moment on my laurels, I took myself to the school where he worked and cajoled him, so to speak, into coming to our center to coordinate the project.

Later, I remembered the little wooden houses I used to see since my childhood days in the countryside, and which always seemed so special to me. Upon entering them, I used to experience a sensation of warmth and well-being that made it difficult for me to leave them. I was aware that in the schools and in the homes there existed, in general terms, a gross lack of this sense of well-being which is so important for the development of the individual. It occurred to me to design a structure that would in no way resemble a formal school, but would possess the necessary elements of human warmth, so that, on entering it, the young people would feel wanted and welcomed. In 1972 we opened the Casa del Balcón, a small wooden country-style house, completely surrounded by a porch. It was the center for the activities of our Project on Alternatives to Formal Education. I wanted to make it so informal that on one occasion, my friend, Gordon Klopf came to visit me and found that the inside walls of the house were bare. He said: "No, no, no; neither too much nor too little. To teach one must illustrate. The experience of learning must be as concrete as possible, so that the children may be able to better internalize the concepts and ideas presented to them." We wasted no time in covering the house with posters and pictures proper to the learning process, and we labeled each accordingly. We even set up a fish tank, with real fish of course.

Another situation we saw in the Playa that required re-education leading to a change in behavior was the stealing and mistreatment of animals. It seems that some young playeros were in the habit of "borrowing" horses belonging to other people without either asking permission or having any intention of returning the horses. They not only stole the animals, but also mistreated them. They used to put paint thinner into their halters and the horses would react by going hysterical and running around wildly, all of which entertained their torturers no end. We were quite upset at this sight, and Néstor conceived the idea of forming a club. We suggested this to the young men, who liked the idea. One of them said: "Yes, we could call it "The Rustler's Club." Then Néstor, with patience and tact, pointed out the inappropriateness of that name—which was a name given to those who stole horses—since they had already begun to lead a very different life style. Little by little, he brought them around and they called it instead the Tabaiba Equestrian Club, and under that name we incorporated it into the Casa del Balcón. By means of the club, they were taught how to take care of and protect "their" horses, and we brought in veterinarians who showed them how harmful the thinner was for the poor animals. Before long, we were able to stop the horse thievery. All of these experiences began to strengthen in the minds of the young people the idea that they had to learn in order to develop their personalities. It was a school in disguise that finally taught them how to develop their capabilities and skills and to love studying.

A building that came to house the program named Center for Alternative Education for Playeros has a very peculiar history. It was a place occupied by a bar called El Tropicana; this bar was a source of concern for us all because it was a center for prostitution. It was sad to see those young women, some almost children, giving themselves over to prostitution in the belief that such was their lot in life. We tried to get the police to intervene and urge the owners to close, but the latter had all their papers in order, and said that the girls were only employees who served drinks and did nothing else. One morning a young woman was found dead in the bar. We could stand the situation no longer, and decided to speak with the woman who owned the property, and from whom the bar's owners rented the building. She said they were good tenants and punctual in paying their rent. We then offered her a higher rent, and she consented to allow us to lease the building. The owners of the bar had to leave, and we took possession of the place in the name of a better future for our youth. We cleaned the place and painted it in festive and bright colors. Then we welcomed young people filled with expectations for a better life and tutors eager to educate them. The person in charge of that first educational endeavor was

Doña Helvetia Nicole, one of the great educators and leaders of the Ponce community.

On another occasion, a rather peculiar event took place. Whenever I used to speak to the playeros, I would always try to convince them that they had the right to a better life than that which they were leading. I remember one night several employees of the Center came to the cenacle to wake me up because a large number of playeros were squatting left and right on lands in the Playa, and were threatening to take over those acres belonging to the Center in the Tabaiba sector. I leapt from my bed and, upon arriving at the place, saw almost all the employees and friends of the Center forming a cordon around our property by linking their arms and thereby forming a human barricade through which no one could pass. I spoke with the leaders of the squatters' group and asked them not to take the places that belonged to the Center. They complied, but instead proceeded to take over other properties, including some that belonged to my family.

I remember very clearly the year 1974. Our dear friend and unconditional collaborator, the attorney Francisco Parra, was always offering us his counsel, not just in legal matters, but also in every aspect of life, since he was a prodigious student of the arts and sciences. He was advising us with respect to the cultivation of the land since the soil of the Playa is arid. He had read that coffee and rice could be cultivated in this zone, and so we set out to cultivate these plants. We experimented with rice, but it never went beyond an experiment because, no sooner had the rice appeared than the local crabs ate it all. (Perhaps we should have taken advantage of the banquet they had enjoyed by throwing them in a cauldron and having a feast of "rice with crabmeat"). At the same time, we began planting coffee and soon gave the project a name: "Jardines del Cafetal." Thanks to the advice of our dear Ico Parra (as we affectionately called him), we initiated a project that today yields great dividends to the youth who participate, and to the Center. We eventually got to the point where we planted 60,000 coffee trees a year.

I remember an incident that happened at the beginning of the project. One morning, while I was walking through the Center as was my custom, I saw a young man seated along the curb with his head bowed down. I approached him and said: "What's your name?"

Without lifting his head, he answered: "Torpedo."

I continued my interrogation: "Torpedo, what's wrong; why aren't you smiling?"

He answered: "How can I smile if I have children to support and have no work?"

Then I said to him: "Well, if that's your problem, we can resolve it right away. Come tomorrow morning to work in the coffee plant nursery." He did so, and a few weeks later, I saw him at the Center with such a radiant expression on his face, that I did not recognize him. Upon seeing me, he called out: "Sister, I can smile now."

I asked: "Who are you?" and he answered: "I'm Torpedo." I marvelled at the way a desperate person can change, even physically, when he is offered an opportunity.

I enjoyed another great satisfaction on another occasion: through the good offices of Ed Miller and Irene Delano, our young photographers were given the great honor of exhibiting their work in New York's Metropolitan Museum of Art. I shall never forget the expressions on their faces: joy, pride, surprise, shyness, incredulity. They were emotions that these youngsters themselves would never forget. It was Feast of the Magi, January 6th. Six of the young playero photographers accompanied by Sister Rosita, Nelson García, Ed Miller, Irene Delano, and me very proudly opened the exhibit. What an emotional moment:

to receive the keys of the City of New York from the hands of Amalia Betanzos who represented the mayor, Abraham Beame! We, on our part, gave them our gift of the Magi: our exhibit of photographs of the young playeros of Ponce. Somehow, the devotion of the Three Kings had transcended the limits of our Puerto Rican tradition. All in all, it was a great experience for our young men who, finding themselves far from their familiar surroundings, were able to experience the fact that their dignity was great no matter where they might go.

Another of the Lord's great blessings was the idea of setting up a place of prayer which we called "el Remanso," and where we placed an image of the Virgin. God blessed us by letting us have our own virgin, our Virgen Playera, created by a local craftsman, José Ermitaño. Her face is fashioned out of clay and her features are those of a playera woman, tanned by the sun and toughened by daily toil. She is crowned with a wreath of coral and algae. He placed the image in a special space, a niche in the shape of a rowboat, symbolic of the work of our fishermen and created by Enrique Téllez, an old fisherman himself. Beneath her feet, a sign reads: "Virgin Mary of the Trinity, our hope, in the name of the fishermen of the Playa and of the entire world, we proclaim you Queen of the Universe." My friend and collaborator, Olga Schuck, wrote words I still remember: "Thus, the rowboat with its prow pointing to the heavens, daring and proud, defies space, as it protects its precious cargo...the most beautiful image of the Virgin...."

The memory of my dear baseball players of Cabo Rojo came back to me when, in 1976, the employees of the Diagnostic and Treatment Center created a softball team and affectionately christened it Los Iso (the "Isos"), an abbreviation of my name. This time it was they themselves who organized the team for fun and exercise, while the

105

"Saints" of Cabo Rojo had been organized by the religious with the goal of attracting its members to the church. But when it came to playing, everything was the same: a positive attitude, great energy, and a desire to have a good time. The basic intention was the same too: to show the people of Cabo Rojo in one case and the playeros in the other that they were people of great worth because of their innate dignity, and that they must live in keeping with that awareness.

The elderly became another cause of concern for me, when I saw that many of them, although retired because the law had set an age for mandatory retirement, were still strong and productive. An idea then occurred to us which we later called "Adoptive Grandparents." Its purpose was to give back a sense of dignity to the many senior citizens who after retirement feel useless and unwanted, with nothing to contribute to their families or to society in general. We brought out from their homes those elderly people who were still able to take care of themselves and were still productive, taking them to places where they could be useful, such as schools, rehabilitation centers for alcohol and drug addicts, and other such locations, and giving them a stipend for services rendered. What a difference this program has made to our grandparents! Their joy permeates every aspect of their lives. They have even formed a dance group to revive the dances of years past, and they themselves have sewn period costumes. They go everywhere, spreading some of their youthful spirit with Puerto Rico's beautiful danzas that can never go out of style. So much can be accomplished with a little love and perseverance.

I have kept a beautiful letter received in 1977 from a good and humble playero which showed me that we were moving in the right direction. Here is a portion of that letter: "...Through you I learned to know what life, hope and love are truly about; I had my first contact with interesting books, my first education....Well, Sister Isolina, my humble condition of greengrocer permits me to offer you as a gift only whatever greens you need, or to teach your young people how to plant the same. P.S. Do not forget that you have an appointment to have lunch with my eight children and my wife...." May God bless Don Juan, the greengrocer, whom I have not seen for many years because of the many obligations in which this whirlwind that is the Center keeps me constantly involved.

On one occasion we had a visit from Rubén Berríos Martínez, president of the Independista Party of Puerto Rico. At the end of his tour of the Center, he remarked: "What you are doing here in the Playa is what I dream for the Republic of Puerto Rico." There is no doubt that any program that supports human dignity above and beyond any other goal is a precious treasure for individuals or groups who desire with all their hearts a better quality of life.

For a long time, my dear friend, singer Danny Rivera, had often visited with me. During his first few visits he just quietly observed us but, little by little, he began to identify himself with our work; gradually my cause, the cause of the playeros, of the people who had nothing, became his as well. Thus, together, we planned many concerts in which he starred for the benefit of the Center. I have always been able to count on his unconditional support.

The struggles between teenage gangs, many of which were secretly directed by big shots from the underworld, have been around for several decades. Puerto Rico is not an exception to the rule, nor is the Playa de Ponce. In the community called Lirios del Sur there emerged a group, supposedly the "defenders" of the defenseless, that called itself "Las Avispas," ("the Wasps"). They roamed about armed to the teeth. Their weapons, as is usually the case, were extremely powerful. Many of them ended up in jail because of the crimes they committed, from assaults to robberies. One day their leader, Joseíto, a young man who, like most young people, had good, but misdirected sentiments, landed in jail. When he was released, Joe, one of the mediators in our advocacy program, spoke to me about him, and I decided to call him to my office. We had a conversation during which he told me about his wife and children, and I pointed out to him his talents for leadership, emphasizing the fact that he could create a better future for himself as well as for his community. Noting that he was open to my words, I offered him a position as janitor in my office located in the building of the Ferré Industries. He took the job and proved to be a very responsible employee with whom I often had the opportunity to chat. I would reiterate my belief in his leadership qualities and suggest how he might help his community. He began to get the message, and a change started to take place in him.

Unfortunately, his enemies could not understand the process through which Joseíto was passing. With his change of heart, and with his desire to change the group, the business of drug sales was going to collapse. Then one afternoon, during an outing in the country, he was murdered. The news traveled quickly, and some of the Wasps came to tell me. I dropped everything. When we arrived at the community center of the Lirios district where he was being waked, I saw that the Wasps were not allowing anyone to enter except for members of their gang or Joseíto's immediate family. The police were stationed outside to maintain order, in fear of a possible riot, since it was not yet known who had caused Joseíto's death. People were saying to us: "Sisters, it's dangerous to try to go in." But we were already there, and we were not about to leave without saying at least an Our Father for his soul. Finally, they allowed us to enter.

We offered our condolences to Joseíto's family and to the members of his leadership team. With great devotion, we all recited the rosary, as is the custom in Puerto Rican wakes. Later, a young man, a member of the Wasps, came over to me and placed on my dress a pin in the shape of a wasp (the symbol of the organization). They did the same with the sisters who had accompanied me, and later proclaimed us "godmothers" of the Wasps.

While the "Wasps" were "acting out" in the Lirios del Sur district, there was another group in the area called El Salistral (the Salt Pans) working under the shadow of another leader named Moncho. He was a "Newyorican," and quite a bit older that Joseíto, but very aggressive, and he exerted great control over the young men of the Salistral. Before long, he was arrested and tried for a crime I do not now recall; he was out on bail, however, until the trial, and decided to pay me a visit. I received him in my office, and when he appeared, I said: "Come in, Moncho, have a seat. And to what do I owe the honor of this visit?"

He sat down and, looking straight into my eyes, went directly to the point: "You and I have something in common."

"Oh really? Tell me, what is it you and I have in common?" I responded calmly.

"You work for your people and they love you and need you," he said; "I work for mine and they also love me and need me. On the other hand, just as there are people who don't like me, there are people who don't like you."

I urged him then to continue in an effort to discover what it was he wanted. Encouraged, he went on: "Just now I'm waiting for my trial and I will most likely go to jail. I need a letter of recommendation from you so as not to leave my people all alone."

I did not turn a hair, although I knew that I might be risking my life by the answer I was about to give him. I stared into his eyes just as he had stared into mine earlier, and said: "We are both equal before God, but we have *nothing* in common because the work I do for my people—and it so happens that some of them are also your people—is that of trying to develop their talents to the utmost so they can become useful members of society, helping both themselves and the community. You, on the contrary, work for yourself and your own perdition, slowly destroying your people and your community; for that end I will not help you."

We remained quiet, staring into each other's eyes and, after a few minutes, he got up and walked silently to the door. Then I said to him: "God bless you, Moncho." He paused without turning his head, listened to my blessing, and left. Later I learned that he was sentenced to a term in jail. Thank God, we were able to rescue many of his friends and gang members who now work with us at the Center.

In contrast to this experience, by the end of the year we had in the Lirios del Sur area the first graduation of forty young people who desired to overcome all obstacles and make something of their lives. In an effort to encourage others from the same district to achieve similar goals, our friend, the singer Danny Rivera, gave a free concert to that community which we all enjoyed very much.

Today my journey has transcended the boundaries of the Playa and has led me to Caimito in Río Piedras, where Sister Teresa Géigel struggles valiantly at another center like that of the Playa. Guayama also has been marked with my already tired footsteps, which Marta Almodóvar follows faithfully in that town.

Recently we celebrated a Congress in which I sought to participate with people from all parts of the island who, like myself, wanted to improve the quality of life of Puerto Rican men and women. We tried to convince everyone that if one acknowledges oneself to be a child of God and a brother or sister to others, one can help them discover their innate dignity, and can also help them develop their potential as human beings. Aware of this, each person can then be drawn into a solid commitment with the community. We helped them see, in other words, that we are all called to be "advocates"; that what we have done, and are doing, in the centers, is an experience that can be duplicated by anyone willing to help their neighbor. All that is required is the desire to work with all one's heart so that the glory of God may be fully manifested in each man and each woman.

AFTERWORD

In the year 1985 I wrote in *El Playero:*

They say that I retired; I have already celebrated my Golden Jubilee—50 years of service—it's time that someone else take up the conductor's baton, and who better than Sister Rosita, the faithful helper who has labored tirelessly at my side, giving constant proofs of her faith, hope and commitment. To confirm this decision, the Lord called me and said: "Sister, leave it all in my hands," and He wounded my heart that it might beat more slowly, and that I might learn to give up everything. I remembered that Gospel reading I had heard long ago in Cuba about Mary Magdalen, the great sinner turned saint who broke the jar of perfume to anoint the feet of Jesus; who broke it because she would no longer use it for things that are not consistent with the following of Jesus. Now, how am I to serve? If my assignment in the past has been "I do and therefore I can," how can I now find the path the Lord is opening to me? It is to be a witness of the love of God to my brethren; what service can be more beautiful?

The word *service* has so many definitions and applications: a mother serves when she rocks her child on her lap; the friend who shares joys and sorrows with a companion, serves; the "Wasps" serve when they collect money for the victims of the landslide in Mameyes; the leader who provides recreation for abandoned street children also serves. We can all serve, even though it be only by a smile which lifts the spirit of anyone who crosses our path. I have served for many years and, with the help of my sisters and companions in the struggle, I have left behind me a permanent work at the service of Puerto Rico. Now it's time for me to leave it in writing in a book that underscores the ideas, the anxieties, the hopes that the Center made possible. And may our motto—"SERVICE IS THE WAY WE SPEAK"— shine ever more brightly.

At this moment of my life, I pause; I stop to look back and gain some perspective. I am surprised to discover a series of "coincidences" that have occurred at certain important moments of my life and that cannot but attract my attention. I remember when, on July 22, 1935 in Havana, Jesus called me to the service of the poor, utilizing the biblical figure of the Magdalen breaking her precious alabaster flask. It was a call that brought a great liberation and transformation into my life.

Later, on another July 22—this time July 22, 1968—God gave me one of the most marvelous gifts I have ever received from Him: he sent me to the Playa of Ponce, and whispered in my ear, as I traveled through his paths: "My Playa shall be your Playa." He turned me into a playera, not only of the Playa de Ponce, but of all those "playas" where only misery and poverty are found....

Finally, one morning as I opened my eyes after a night's rest at the home of my dear nephew Maurice, in Miami, I felt a sharp pain in my chest. I decided to get up and walk about the garden, but the pain did not leave my heart. It was 6:30 on the morning of July 22, 1985, and suddenly I lost my awareness of things, until I awakened in a hospital bed. I remember seeing the friendly face of Dr. Raúl García Rinaldi. His words to me were: "Isolina, don't worry, I have to open your heart so that you can continue your journey. All you have to do is pray." He kept his word; his medical knowledge, in perfect coordination with his healing hands and his great faith in God, put my feet back on the road of my life.

These coincidences that I discover today are just that, mere coincidences—which turn into extraordinary events when I seek and find God in them. Those readers who believe in destiny may chart a certain future for me on the basis of them; I do not. I simply have no time to chart future expectations for my life. I believe in the Providence of God, who opens our spiritual eyes to the everyday circumstances of our daily living so that we can see beyond the horizon, not in a fatalistic way but in a positive manner, so we can draw from life the best that it has to offer. I live in the present, believing that the steps I am taking at this moment affect those who walk alongside me in a positive way. I do not worry about the future. God, in whom I have trusted since childhood, will take care of that.

The men or women who have met God on their journey enjoy the great blessing of looking back and being fully aware of the footprints He has left on the paths of their lives. In this retrospective glance, I can see with humble joy how God touched my life through my beloved mother. When I was a child neither she, nor much less I who was so small, were aware of what God was preparing within me: the birth of a vision that moved me to dedicate part of my youth to helping others, and that eventually led me to the religious life, that I might go with joy wherever I was sent, to serve the poorest of the poor. All those acts of charity she performed for the poor, those conversations we shared, and the lessons she taught in making me share the best that I had with those who were least materially privileged were her legacy to me. I also see my father, so concerned about the beggars he met and chatting with them like an old friend. I remember my naive fears concerning my brothers' salvation as I heard them talk about Voltaire and his ideas; yet, later, all of them would offer their unconditional support in all the many undertakings in which I would become involved. Neither can I forget the Religious of the Sacred Heart who taught me how to love the elderly. I remember how, after my mother's death, my heart burned with the desire to imitate her by helping poor people and young men seeking employment, as well as the shoeshine boys and the newspaper vendors.

I see clearly my first contacts with the Missionary Servants of the Most Blessed Trinity, and the honor of having been guided by that congregation's founder, Father Thomas Augustine Judge. It was he who, in great measure, helped me to clarify my vocation and my vision of helping the poorest. Across the years, his prophetic words have always illumined my path, like a North Star in the firmament of my life: "The Almighty Designer has a life plan for you, and on each of your days his mysterious Providence is weaving everything into a work of incomparable beauty...Daughter, God needs you to help the many poor children there are in Puerto Rico."

Today I continue the journey. To what goal? I do not know; only God knows. It is He who moves the motor of my life. I do not know why I cannot stop; there seems to be a superior force that impels my fragile body forward. I am resigned to that now, and I do not resist it. I do not hold back, because even when I take my customary walk through the facilities of the Center in Tabaiba, I feel a great satisfaction in seeing all that my companions and I have achieved with the playeros. At the same time I get a bubbling feeling within me which says: "This chapter is not yet closed." It is not closed because, although my mortal nature may slow my steps and I must in the end disappear from the picture, there is a new generation that has been bitten by the same bug, and they will not be held back.

I felt surer than ever of this the other day when, as I walked through the Center, I heard some noise coming from the meeting room and I peeked in curiously. Then I saw a young woman who asked to address the group and said: "I am a playera, and when I was a child I watched all of you, and Sister Isolina and the other sisters, as you worked hard to make us understand that we playeros had great dignity. Little by little I internalized that message and decided to study social work so I could come here to the Center and tell you that I am here to give back by my service all the support and the trust that my family and I received here." Testimonies such as this are carved into my memory and my heart as a gentle incentive to let go and offer no resistance when the Beloved of my heart whom I love above all other loves comes to take me home, where I shall never more be separated from Him.

On a certain occasion, while standing on a platform, I looked out at my brothers and sisters of the Playa, and I felt very tiny as I saw the great miracle that surrounded me: the faith, the struggle, the tenacity of those who serve and are served so that they might come to recognize their self worth, and make an effort, and triumph. And I saw all that, with the liveliness of the joyful music, as the playeros congratulated one another. Today, with each drum beat of my heart—while I continue walking, observing, and rejoicing in the glory of God manifested in the plenitude of these men and the women—I give thanks to God for having allowed me to serve a people who are so worthy and so good.